Land of Dreams

By the same author:

Moon in the Pail (novel)
The Rabbi and the Nun (novel)
Begin's Life and Legacy (with Hillel Seidman)
Federman's Travels (biography)
Guide for Translators (reference, under pen-name)
The Translator's Handbook (reference, under pen-name)

Translations:

Sparks of Glory (Holocaust stories by Moshe Prager)
Wanted (Lehi memoir by Yaacov Eliav)
From Darkness to Light (Chabad memoir by Benjamin Gorodetzk

LAND
OF
DREAMS

An Israeli Childhood

Mordecai Schreiber

Shengold Books

Schreiber Publishing, Inc.
P. O. Box 2142
Rockville MD 20847 USA

Shengold Books is an imprint of Schreiber Publishing

First Printing

Publisher's Cataloging-in-Publication

Schreiber, Mordecai
        Land of Dreams: an Israeli Childhood / Mordecai Schreiber
        p. cm.
        Preassigned LCCN: 97-65719
        ISBN: 1-887563-39-3

        1. Schreiber, Mordecai. 2. Haifa (Israel). 3. Israel
--History. I. Title.

DS10.H3S34 1997   956.946'052
                                   QBI97-40439

Perhaps it never happened
Perhaps
I never rose at dawn
To till the soil with the sweat of my brow.

Did I ever, on long sweltering
Harvest days
From atop a wagon laden with sheaves
Break into song?

Did I ever cleanse myself in the calm blue,
In the purity
of my Kinneret... oh, my Sea of Galilee,
Was it you, or was it only a dream?

Rachel, 1927

FORETHOUGHT

Once there was an eight-year-old boy who witnessed a very
unusual birth. It was not the birth of a person but of a country.
It took about three years for that country to be born. Nearly half
a century later, the author, who was once that child, embarked on
a journey to rediscover that boy and what he went through during
that birth and its aftermath. In the following pages the boy and
the man tell us about the experience of the birth, or perhaps the
rebirth of this country.

PART I:

THE DREAM

1.

When I was eight years old the state of Israel was born. It was a most unusual event. Most people -- be they French, Haitian, Turkish -- are born long after their country of birth has been in existence. To be an eight-year-old child and watch your own country's birth is something extraordinary. Particularly when people like your parents and their parents and their parents' parents, going back nearly two thousand years, dreamed of this event and prayed for it to happen all their lives. Yes, even at the tender age of eight I knew all about those "two thousand years." They were drummed into our heads even before we started kindergarten, day in, day out. Every time we were told to stand up and sing the *Hatikva,* the song that would become our national anthem, we concluded with the words,

> *Our hope is not yet lost,*
> *The two-thousand-year-old hope,*
> *To become a free people in our own land,*
> *The land of Zion and Jerusalem.*

During my childhood I must have heard that number, "two thousand years," at least a million times. It was invariably followed by some eloquent Zionist statement, such as, "For the first time in two thousand years we have our own policemen." By the time I was a teenager my friends and I swore never to use this number again, except in jest.

But the birth of the state was no jest. First, you had to wonder why were you so lucky to be the one witnessing the birth, when so many before you never lived to see it. Were you better than they? Were you more deserving? Next you would wonder whether this state was really what they had all dreamed of and prayed for for so long. And then you went through life trying to define yourself and understand what had happened to you.

I have now spent nearly fifty years trying to come to terms with what that eight-year-old went through during and after the birth of the state. My entire life has been shaped by that event. No doubt, it was one of the most extraordinary events in all of history. Nothing quite like it has ever happened before or since. Where else did a people return to its historical land after twenty centuries of exile? Where else was an ancient language brought back to life, to become one of today's most dynamic and creative languages? Where else did a people oppressed and persecuted and homeless, reenter the stage of history, strong and youthful and proud? Was I really part of that miracle? Was I really a witness to the birth?

Yes, I was.

As a child, I recall taking pride in the fact I was named after the only person in the Bible referred to specifically as "the Jew." No one else in the Bible, except for Mordecai, Queen Esther's cousin and foster father, is called "the Jew." I had no doubt I was a descendant of the biblical Mordecai, since the Bible tells us he was a Benjaminite, and all the Benjaminites were left-handed, and so am I. What's more, Mordecai saved the Jews from perishing in the hands of Haman the Wicked, and somehow I felt I was destined to save the Jews just like he did. This was apparently my great childhood fantasy.

Talking about fantasies, all little Jewish girls at some point are dressed on Purim as Queen Esther, and all little Jewish boys as some Jewish hero, be it Mordecai, or Judah Maccabee, or a more recent hero, who saved his people. In this respect my

10

fantasy was not altogether unusual. What was unusual was the fact that I took such pride in being called "the Jew." In my native Haifa around the time of the birth of the state, people preferred to call themselves Hebrews rather than Jews. Jews were people who spoke Jewish, or Yiddish. They lived in Europe and were persecuted. Here in this renewed land people became once again Hebrews who spoke the ancient Hebrew tongue. I had no difficulty understanding this concept, and I considered myself very fortunate to be a Hebrew who spoke the same language Mordecai spoke. But for some reason which I cannot explain, I was not ready to give up my exclusive biblical title, "the Jew."

They say some people are born out of place and time. I often felt that way about myself. I think of how I was born in the most tragic year in my people's history -- 1939, the year Hitler invaded Poland and started the massacre that would eventually wipe out nearly every relative I've ever had. I was an infant at the time and I couldn't do a thing to save them. And I also think of how in 1947 I was only eight years old, when I should have been at least eighteen, old enough to fight in my people's war of survival and independence. Not to mention the fact that when I tried to see action in Israel's later wars I was told I was too old.

But one thing they can never take away from me. As a child, I saw the land of my people come back to life. It was the most extraordinary thing that ever happened to anyone on this earth. That one moment, the birth of my country Israel, was worth living and dying for. And I know that even if I live to be a thousand, there will never be anything like it again. And now, nearly half a century later, I would like to revisit that moment, go back to that place and time and tell you what it was like to be there. But before I do, I must first rediscover myself, find that eight year old child who lived in Haifa almost fifty years ago, and

11

all the people and the events of those days he can still remember.

2.

In 1947 I lived on a one-block street on the edge of the lower city of Haifa, called Rehov Luntz, with my parents and my four-year-old sister. As a second grader, I recall coming home one day from school with my report card. My mother was standing on the street corner when I arrived. She took my report card and her face turned red.

"Two B's," she snapped. "How come?"

I shrugged.

"Two B's," she repeated. It sounded as though I had committed an unspeakable crime.

I gritted my teeth.

Before I knew it, she pulled me by my sleeve and slapped me on my ear.

"It's the last time you are going to bring home B's, you hear me?"

I looked down at my sandals. From that day on I only brought home A's and A+'s. My mission in life was not to embarrass my mother, but rather make her proud of me. I was the apple of her eye. I was all she lived for, so how could I let her down?

Years later, as I was finishing high school, I finally rebelled against grades. It started to dawn on me I had other interests in life besides getting straight A's. But that was much later. In 1947 everything was different. All of us, regardless of age, had a special mission in life. We were out to prove we could do great and unusual things, each one of us in his or her own way. We were giving birth to a nation, and we had to prove in any way possible we were capable and worthy of performing such a miracle. For me, an eight-year-old who started out in life as a bookworm, it meant getting straight A's. That was my assigned

13

task, my mission. So I put my mind to it and I did it.

The best way to describe myself and my peers in those days is by saying we were good little soldiers. We were even dressed like soldiers, in khaki shorts and khaki shirts. We were encouraged to engage in every form of outdoor activity, such as long hikes, soccer and basketball, wrestling, swimming, and so on. While I enjoyed all those activities, my greatest interest was knowledge. There never seemed to be enough books around for me to read. To paraphrase Bacon, I made all knowledge my province, which made me a model student, the kind of student teachers dream of and other students openly admire and secretly resent.

My studiousness earned me the name "Reb Mordheh," the familiar Yiddish way of saying "Rabbi Mordecai."

Haifa as my father and mother saw it in 1931

Haifa today

With my parents, Haifa, 1940

In 1947, the year Israel's birth began,
with my sister, Dahlia

My father (back row, far right), among the
first recruits of the Air Force

The whole family, including my little sister,
Sani, at Hof Hacarmel (Carmel Beach), 1954

With Menachem Begin in Cleveland, Ohio, 1970

With my sisters, Dahlia (right) and Sani, some
fifty years after the birth of the state

At my daughter Marla's wedding with the Israeli
and the American families

3.

Little *Reb Mordheh* was a rather good looking kid. The reason I know this is because around the time Israel was born my parents took me to the photo shop on Herzl Street for some sit-down pictures with my three-year-old sister, Dahlia. One of those pictures was placed in the show window and remained there for months. In those days I could only think of Dahlia as a nuisance and a misfortune. But looking back it's quite possible the real nuisance was I. Dahlia later on became a great beauty, probably one of the most beautiful women in Israel. Even now, in her early fifties, men on the street still turn their heads when she passes by. I must say we were quite a pair, those two kids in the picture, and to use the self-deprecating Jewish expression of that time, "we looked like Gentiles."

As I look at this now yellowing picture, I wonder what that seven or eight year old child was all about. I learned later on the child had been carefully planned. No accident he. He was preceded, I was once told, by one abortion and one miscarriage. By the time he arrived on the scene all the economic, social and ideological reasons for him to be born had been worked out. He was going to be the New Person, the New Jew, yet to be properly named. Some day they would call him "Israeli."

What kind of a new person did the child's parents seek to create? Many seem to think they had in mind a superior type, a "Super-Jew," if you will. A Jewish version of the German *Übermensch* which the German National Socialists sought to create in the thirties. Nothing is farther from the truth. They sought to create a normal, ordinary person. They had decided to leave Europe because they felt Jews in early twentieth century Europe had reached an extreme state of abnormality. They and their friends felt they were strangers in their own land. They

15

were not free to live where they wanted or choose the kind of work they wanted to do, but were restricted to certain areas and to a few occupations no one else wanted. To make matters worse, they had been chained by their own religious life which their rabbis had created, removing them almost completely from any normal daily activities, into a world completely dominated by religious strictures, "thou shalt not" this and "thou shalt not" that. By the time the child's parents were sixteen or seventeen they felt, separately and similarly, they were being frozen into a futureless existence, and they started finding breathing difficult.

It was around that time in their young life they decided to go elsewhere and start a new life. Unlike millions of immigrants who left Europe in those years -- Jews, Catholics, Lutherans and others -- the child's parents had a much more ambitious plan. Almost an impossible dream. They wanted to become normal Jews. Not just normal, mind you. To become normal they could have gone somewhere else, like, for instance, America, and become Americans. They specifically wanted to become normal Jews. Jews who could do all the things other people do, good and bad. Jews without outside or self-imposed strictures. And, when the child was ready to come into the world, they wanted him to be a normal child, a child who could do anything, become anything, take his own destiny into his own hands. This is basically all they wanted for him. They wanted him to be the first Jew in two thousand years, since Rome destroyed Jerusalem, who lived in a free Jewish country. That was the dream. For that dream they were willing to live a life of hardship, give up their own lives if necessary. They were obsessed with this dream. It became all consuming. It was the one thing life was worth living for. And they transmitted the dream to the child.

The funny thing is, they had the good sense to realize the

dream was a folly, even after it was fulfilled. They told the child at a rather young age (they told him many things at a rather young age; in those days they treated young children like fully grown adults) the dream was a folly, a complicated and difficult burden they had laid upon themselves and upon him and his generation, for which they felt quite guilty, and always seemed anxious to make amends for. They were basically simple folks, yet they were very complicated people. And they wanted a simple thing out of life -- to have children and grandchildren and great grandchildren who would live normal lives, play ball, go to the movies, fall in love, choose whatever career that struck their fancy, and, above all else, live as free people in their own free land.

4.

How did I feel when my mother slapped me because I brought home two B's on my report card? I felt grateful. I knew she was right. I should have worked harder than I did. I could have done better and I had no business getting B's. After all, my mother did not have the opportunity to pursue regular studies in Europe because her parents were poor hasidim who did not think a girl needed too much schooling, and even if they did, they could not afford to send her to school. My mother was a very gifted child. When her brother, ignoring his father's prohibition, recited to her a poem by the great Hebrew poet, Bialik, she remembered every word, although she had just started to learn Hebrew with a tutor, and she could even recite that poem backwards. She had the most beautiful handwriting I've ever seen, and she told me she once asked her father why girls could not be Torah scribes, for which she was slapped on both cheeks.

No, my mother did not appreciate being slapped by her father, nor did she appreciate being a second-class Jew because of her gender, and least of all being a second-class citizen in Poland because of her origins. Which is why she left home at nineteen and went to Eretz Yisrael. She believed her father was wrong, and she had the Holocaust to prove it. But I believed she was right, because had she stayed in Europe I would have been become another statistic of the Master Race. My mother had earned her right to slap me, and, looking back, I feel she should have done it more often, for I would have been the better for it. But she didn't, because, after all, she did love me like only a woman who was basically unhappy in her marriage can love her son, to whom she transferred the love she should have given her husband, my father. Slapping me must have caused her great pain, and she only did it when she felt it was absolutely necessary.

5.

Land of dreams. My mother, obviously, was a dreamer. She was also a rebel. Think about it -- a nineteen year girl from a respectable ultra-orthodox home chooses to give up religion, take the train to Constanta -- Romania's seaport on the Black Sea -- to sail to the Middle East and live in a tent, in the middle of the desert, with other nineteen and twenty-two year olds who believe in free love à la Marxist Russia, in living out of wedlock years before it became fashionable in the West, in making their own rules, in working as day laborers and doing any job imaginable for pennies, and dream impossible dreams about picking up where the Bible had left off more than twenty centuries ago.

But what about my father? He was not exactly a dreamer, and certainly not a rebel. What's more, he was a real mamma's boy, very attached to his mother, whom he adored. How did he ever get there? And how did he last all those years in that land which he would sometimes refer to as "a land that eats its inhabitants alive?"

Here it gets very complicated. I really don't have an answer, except to say, perhaps, that there are many unanswered questions about that land of dreams. The best I can do is say that there is something seductive about that land. When that thin tall youth with the shock of blond hair and clear blue eyes who would some day become my father first arrived in that land he was physically seduced by it, and he would never recover. He was still very attached to his mother, and he was yet to meet my mother who would hold on to him for the rest of his life. He was torn between his love for this land and his love for his mother, and he came up with an interesting solution, and to the best of my knowledge this is a true story in all its details, strange as it may sound.

In those days -- the early thirties -- Jewish immigration to Palestine was limited by the British Mandate to a few thousands a year, when many more young Jews in Central and Eastern Europe were looking for ways to reach the Promised Land. Jews had to think of all sorts of clever ways to bring over more fellow Jews than the number of Certificates His Majesty's Government was willing to grant. One such way was fictitious marriages. And so, my father became a fictitious Don Juan. He would go back to Poland every few months, straight back to his village in southern Poland, "marry" one of his former girlfriends, and bring her over to Palestine. Once the newly-weds arrived they would start fighting and get a divorce. The unhappy young man would go right back to Poland and find another wife. This took place four or five times, and as a result four or five young women -- I am not sure of the exact number -- were able to settle in such places as Raanana, Haifa, Tel Aviv and Kfar Yehoshua, and give rise to some fine families. My father, by the way, assured me once he had never taken advantage of any of his "wives," although, who knows, he was certainly a very attractive young man.

6.

My early childhood was as abnormal as can be, but to me, of course, it was perfectly normal. A child does not have a past against which to measure things as "normal" or "abnormal." What you see is what you get, to use the American saying. I imagine a child born and raised in a bordello considers his or her life to be perfectly normal, and may find it difficult to understand what ordinary family life is all about.

I was partially raised in a bomb shelter. The years were 1940, 41, 42. England was at war with Germany and its allies, which included Italy. Mussolini's war planes tried to bomb the British oil refineries and harbor installations in Haifa, which meant that I had the great good fortune of being born in a very strategic town. Many a night my parents had to pull me out of my crib in our second floor apartment and take me down to the cinderblock and cement bomb shelter on the ground floor. I am told Haifa was never hit by Italian bombs, since the Italian pilots were not too interested in Hitler's war and preferred to drop their bombs in the Mediterranean Sea rather than risk their lives by exposing themselves to British anti-aircraft guns.

The real war was being fought elsewhere, in places like Dunkirk, Stalingrad, Pearl Harbor, and Hiroshima. The real victims were not I and my folks in that strip of land along the Mediterranean. The real victims were all the relatives my parents had left behind in Europe. The ones whom the British had refused Certificates. The ones who did not want Certificates because they believed God wanted the Jews to stay in Europe and wait for the messiah. And the ones who felt the best solution to the Jewish problem was assimilation, become gentiles, and disappear among the gentiles once and for all.

The thought of that little baby in the bomb shelter in Haifa in June, 1941, the month the Master Race's trucks and panzers rolled into my mother's and father's villages in Poland, pulled my grandparents whom I had never met and all my uncles and aunts, my cousins and their families, and all their neighbors, teachers and rabbis, pulled them out of their homes and dragged them into the fields and made them dig long trenches and then machine gunned them and turned them into heaps of butchered human flesh, and then covered them with dirt and in effect turned them into a fertilizer, men, women and children, mostly humble souls who did not have the guts my mother had or the cunning my father had, simple souls who believed the Germans were civilized people, who believed God was good, who, even in the face of death, waited for a miracle; the thought of that little baby -- me -- at that moment in time, fills me with the deepest anguish and despair, and as I think of it my heart breaks all over again as it has a million -- no, six million -- times before, and as it will continue to break till the day I die.

But at the same time I hear all those voices, the voices I never knew and yet even now, years later, can hear so clearly, all those beloved voices of my people -- my sweet, darling little Jews, who went to the trenches not to fight but to die, I hear their voices whisper in their sweet Jewish tongue, the language they call Yiddish, a language sweeter than honey, Let the child live. Let Mordecai live for all the Mordecais they took away. Let this land live for all of us who never reached her shores. Let her live forever.

7.

But that was much later. It would take years for an eight-year-old to even begin to grasp what had happened in Europe. No, the adults in that land of dreams did not dwell on those events (is this the right word -- events?) They couldn't dwell on death and dying when they were busy giving birth to nothing less than a new country, a new people, against all odds. It will be interesting to see how they related to the survivors of the Great Destruction when those began to arrive soon after the birth of the state. More on this later.

Where was I the day the state was born? I recall a brilliant sunny day in November, Indian Summer, perhaps. I went to the movies that afternoon with some friends. The movie was called *Fiesta*, and it starred Esther Williams, the lady in the swimsuit who could do amazing things above and under water. The movie was not particularly memorable, since I hardly remembered any of it the moment we left the theater. The movie theater happened to be Orah, on Herzl Street, Haifa's main thoroughfare. In late afternoon Herzl was always a busy street, with people hurrying in all directions, paying little attention to one another. This time, however, it was different. No one was rushing anywhere. People seemed to be most interested in one another. People were seeking out other people, shaking their hands, embracing them, even kissing one another, and here and there there were small circles of people dancing in the middle of the street, stopping traffic.

As I walked down Herzl toward home I began to piece together what was happening. Some very important organization, which represented most of the countries of the world, had taken a vote and decided that the country where I lived, officially known under the British Mandate as Palestine-Land of Israel, was to be partitioned into two new countries -- an Arab Palestine and a Hebrew Land of Israel. That meant that the British would soon leave, and we the Hebrews will become a free people.

Practically from the day I could perceive anything I knew my parents and everyone else around me dreamed of this moment. It was the fulfillment of everyone's dream. It was clearly an event of unprecedented importance. It was so monumental that for young children like me it was something beyond our comprehension. What did it really mean? What was life going to be like from now on? I began to imagine all sorts of things. We were all going to be rich and powerful. We children would have all our wishes fulfilled. The adults would stop complaining about this and that, and everyone would go around loving one another.

But then came the day after. It was a typical November day, cloudy with a hint of rain. All the children in my elementary school were gathered in the school yard for an assembly. Our principal, Yair Katz, was choked with emotion. I don't quite remember what he said, but I do remember one of my friends raised his hand and asked, "Does all of this mean that now the messiah has come?"

My second grade teacher, Ephratya, asked the principal for permission to answer the question. "Children, she said, this is a great and wonderful day, but it is certainly not the time of the messiah. Unfortunately, the Arabs refuse to go along with the decision, and they are threatening to start a war against us. We are bracing ourselves for a very difficult time ahead. But we are hoping for the best."

Quite frankly, she left me baffled. Why would people dance in the streets and hug and kiss one another if they were heading for some very difficult times? Adults, I noted, were very puzzling creatures, full of contradictions. Finally when the day they had all been dreaming of all their lives had arrived, they seemed to be more worried than ever before.

8.

Suffering was all around me. The joy and ecstasy of the birth of the state was mixed with a huge dosage of suffering. Even as an eight-year-old who had little to compare life against, I felt it vividly, more than I could tell at the time. It is amazing, looking back, how desperately everyone tried to keep up a semblance of normality, particularly for the sake of the children, who should not be traumatized by the daily events and by what was yet to come. We now read about life in the Warsaw Ghetto under the Germans, when schools were run in the face of death, a Purim play put on, new Yiddish songs written. It is perfectly understandable. And, perhaps, it is the Jewish thing to do, celebrate life no matter what, even in hell.

The day after that school assembly we started getting news about Jews being killed by Arabs near Tel Aviv, in Jerusalem, and elsewhere. My parents, who in the past avoided talking about the British rule, were now speaking openly about it, about how the British were allowing all this to happen, and, indeed, were even encouraging it. The British, my parents were saying, were out to prove that the Jews could not rule themselves. Certainly not with all that Arab opposition. The Jews were better off having them, the British, protect them. But as the Good Book says, the Jews are a stiff-necked people who refuse to listen to reason.

You wait and see, the British were saying, the Jews will come back and beg us to return and save them from the Arabs. This UN decision is sheer nonsense. Those UN delegates are not familiar with this part of the world. They will soon find out.

The British, it seemed, managed to throw a very menacing word at the Yishuv, as we the Jews of Palestine were known in those days. The word was "chaos," better yet, *tohu vavohu*, the expression used in the second verse of the book of Genesis to describe the condition of the universe before creation ("And the land was *tohu vavohu*, namely, void and chaos, and there was darkness over the face of the deep.") As a child the word made a deep impression on me. Only a few days earlier we children thought the messiah had arrived, and here we were told we were facing chaos, a total breakdown of law and order, followed by death and destruction.

It was a very somber time.

And here I must introduce a very important player from the drama of those days, namely, my father's truck. Out of context it may sound quite ludicrous. First, what has a truck got to do in the middle of all those momentous events? A truck is a common ordinary vehicle no one ever pays any special attention to. A truck driver is not exactly a romantic figure in the minds of most people. But in Haifa in 1948 it was a different story altogether. Very few people in those days owned a truck, or any other vehicle, for that matter, especially in Haifa, which was a city of working people, factory workers and harbor workers who belonged to the big labor union, the Histadrut. Owning a truck made my father a capitalist in the eyes of his friends and coworkers, and being a truck driver was a much better way of making a living than was available to most.

The truck was an old Ford purchased from U.S. Army surplus after World War Two, with the help of some relatives in America. The story of my childhood is intimately intertwined with that old Ford. In Haifa harbor in the forties and fifties, the Ford and its driver were a familiar sight. My father would drive his truck to the harbor whenever a fishing boat belonging to one of the nearby kibbutzim brought in a harvest of fish from the Mediterranean. The brawny kibbutzniks would help load the

28

crates of fish on the truck, and father would drive back through the Arab quarter to the refrigerated warehouse near our home on Sirkin Street, which was part of Shuk Talpiot, the large indoor market in Haifa. There the fish were sorted out, cleaned, packed in ice, and reloaded on my father's truck to be shipped to markets around the country, from Afulah and Tiberias in the north, to Tel Aviv and Jerusalem in the south.

Single-handedly, my father ran the country's fish distribution, and as such held the key to a most unusual activity, as I was to find out in later years. Working out of Haifa harbor, this affable, mild mannered, law abiding British subject managed to conduct a complicated smuggling operation under the noses of the British harbor police. It all started when the Haganah, the Jewish defense organization, realized the potential of my father's relationship with the British personnel at the harbor. The British, you see, love fish. My father, to stay on their good side, would always put aside some fish for the officials in charge of security at the harbor, especially such species as catfish, which are not kosher, and have little currency in Jewish kitchens.

Soon the Haganah, to which my father belonged from the day he arrived in the land, came up with a scheme. Since the British had made it illegal for the Haganah to own arms, and since the Haganah knew that as soon as Jewish sovereignty was established the Arabs would start shooting, a complicated program of smuggling arms and ammunition into the land was organized in Europe and in America. But how do you smuggle weapons into a country surrounded by hostile Arab neighbors? Obviously, by sea. In those days, the long Mediterranean coast of Israel only had one major harbor, Haifa. Anything of any weight or size had to arrive through Haifa harbor. Jewish fishing boats would rendezvous with foreign freighters out at sea and pay cold cash for rifles, rounds of ammunition, and even mortars and machine guns. The valuable cargo would be hidden at the bottom of fish crates, and brought to the harbor. There it would be loaded on my father's truck underneath several layers of legitimate fish crates. My father would drive up to the main gate of the harbor on Kings Street, and offer the guards two or three choice, plump catfish, or, if the pickings were slim, a handful of sardines. The Limeys' eyes would light up, my father would smile knowingly, and the love affair between him and the guards would be reestablished. No wonder my father always spoke to me in affectionate terms about the British who ruled our land in those days. He and they got along famously. Even during the darkest hours immediately before and after the birth of the state, when the Irgun and the Lehi were blowing up the refineries in Haifa Bay, laying mines on Kings Street and elsewhere and blowing up British jeeps and armor, my father and the British were the best of pals. They loved fish. He loved smuggling guns out of the harbor. Everyone got exactly what they wanted.

9

Back to the truck. Clearly, it was no ordinary truck. It should occupy a place of prominence in the annals of this land. If it could talk, it would tell you a thousand stories. Some happy, some sad. I am sorry I never asked my father to record any of those stories, but I do recall a few, and here are some, starting with what happened to the truck the day after the UN vote on a Jewish state.

In November 1947, the month the famous vote was taken, Haifa -- which stretches from the harbor in the north to the peaks of Mount Carmel in the south, and from the Bay of Zebulun in the east to Bat Galim and the coast in the west -- was a checkerboard of Arab and Jewish neighborhoods. If the white squares were Arab, then the black squares were Jewish. You couldn't mix up the neighborhoods more thoroughly no matter how hard you tried. We lived at the time on Luntz Street, and the street below us was the beginning of the Arab neighborhood. The day after that vote, Jews and Arabs began to draw up their lines of defense in the streets. One line ran less than one hundred yards down the street from us. Behind that line, on top of some of the Arab houses, sniper positions were set up, and I was not allowed to cross that street (Sokolov Street), to reach the next street, Barzilai, where my friend Micha lived.

If you did cross over to Barzilai, you reached the end of the street where the large *Beit Hata'asiya* (Industrial House) was. You turned left down a winding street and reached a beautiful stone bridge running over Wadi Rushmiya, and connecting Haifa with the bay, the Valley of Zebulun, the Emek, and the Galilee. Wadi Rushmiya was a major Arab community, with stone houses clinging to the hills on all sides. This area was one of the strongholds of the Arab irregular forces, or gangs, as we called

31

them. On the other side of the bridge stood a three-story stone building (it is still standing there to this day, with a bronze commemorative plaque marking it as a historical site). It was known to us as the Najada House, and it served as a stronghold for the Arab forces in the eastern neighborhoods of Haifa.

The day after the vote my father had to drive his truck over that bridge to bring fish to the Jewish population on the other side of Haifa Bay, and, more important, to prove that food supplies from Haifa to the hinterland had not been cut off.

He left home before daybreak, and managed to reach his destination unscathed. Around noon he had to come back. He reached the bridge when he started hearing what he recognized to be the bursts of British rifles and a British Bren machine gun, which had been supplied to the Arabs by some British sources. He lowered his head barely above the dashboard and pressed on the gas as hard as he could. He could hear the bullets smashing into his truck's bed, cab, and hood. Holding his breath, he found himself on the other side of the bridge, near Industry House, unharmed.

I was home from school when he walked in the door. I was eight years old. He took me outside and told me he was going to show me something, but I must not say a word to mother about it, since you don't tell women about such things, it could make them very upset.

He showed me the bullet holes in the hood, the trunk, and the side of the truck. Your father is a very lucky man, he told me. He picked me up and held me in his strong arms. "This is our secret," he whispered in my ear. "No one is to know about it except you and me."

I assured him I wouldn't tell anyone, but a week later I did tell my mother, who informed me she already knew about it.

But, as I said, there was a lot more to that truck than smuggling arms and getting hit by bullets. There was the everyday, easy-going side, which I truly loved. I recall those Saturday mornings in the summer, before and after the birth of the state, when we would go on an outing in my father's truck. In our neighborhood no one owned a car, and the only motorized vehicle other than the city bus in our part of Haifa was my father's old middle-sized Ford truck, which the British called "lorry." On hot summer weekends everyone wanted to go to Bat-Galim, where one could choose between the pool and the beach, or farther out to Khayat Beach, the open sea resort.

Getting to the beach by means of my father's truck was never a simple matter. First, my father had to be available. Most weekends he was on an emergency call, transporting the fish from the harbor to Tel Aviv or Jerusalem. In those days there were no refrigerator trucks in Haifa, and unless the fish were transported right after they were pulled out of the Mediterranean, the housewives waiting to prepare gefilte fish and other Jewish delicacies might be disappointed. So all week I would pray for a miracle, namely, no emergency fish transport on the day of rest.

This time my prayer was answered. There was no delivery. As for the sun shining that day, that was no problem, since the sun always shines in Haifa during the summer. Father, as usual, was tired from driving all week, delivering fish crates, and wanted to sleep late. So I made sure to drop a few pots and pans in the kitchen sink to wake him up. This type of activity would usually result in mother leaving a few red fingermarks on my rear end. This time, however, mother was in agreement with my actions, and pretended not to hear. Father muttered a Russian curse in the bedroom, and then slowly got out of bed. Once he got into the bathroom, the familiar ritual of mother goading him to hurry up started. They would go at it for about ten minutes when he finally emerged from the bathroom, red faced and disheveled, and would sit down for a breakfast of yoghurt and toast.

By the time we left the house it was close to nine o'clock in the morning. We now had to make three or four stops along the way to pick up some of father's coworkers from Tnuvah, the food distributing cooperative, whom he had invited to come along on the outing. Not to invite them would have been inconceivable. They expected to be invited. It was the right thing to do. They did not own a car, and they lived on a small salary. Even bus fare was a luxury for them. Besides, one went out in a group, so that the children could play together, and the adults could sit on the sand and talk politics.

So the three of us got into the cab of the truck, and father started the engine, when we heard someone shouting.

We turned around to look. It was Nisim, our neighbor, who was barely on speaking terms with us. Father tried to pretend he didn't hear him, but Nisim's voice was so loud it could wake up the dead. Still, father pretended he didn't hear. Nisim was not about to give up. He dashed in front of the truck, waving his hands.

Father craned his head and looked out of the window.

"What's the matter?"

"Shame on you," Nisim protested, my family and I are suffocating in our ground floor apartment, and here you are going to the beach."

"So what do you want me to do?" father asked, playing dumb. "Stay home and suffocate with you?"

"You have plenty of spare room on the truck."

"I am picking up twenty people."

34

"So you make it twenty two."

By now Nisim's wife and her three little children were parading alongside the truck, fully equipped for the beach. I did some quick arithmetic. Nisim and his family were five. That would make twenty-five, not twenty-two. Besides, Nisim's wife was so big she seemed to fill up half of the truck by herself.

"Don't say anything," my father told my mother, noticing the angry glint in her eye. "It's no big deal."

He got off the truck, unhooked the tailgate, and let Nisim and his family on the truck. Nisim hurled his children onto the truck bed, as father and he took hold of each of Nisim's wife's elbows and hoisted her aloft. Father returned to the cab and we rolled down the street to pick up Moishe Futterman and his family.

What I was afraid of was that by the time we picked up everyone it would be time to go home and we would miss going to the beach. Sure enough, no one was ready when we got there, even though we were already over an hour late. Like my father, they all wanted the best of both worlds. On the one hand, they all wanted to go to the beach. But at the same time they wanted to sleep as late as possible.

By the time we did our last pickup, which happened to be Fritz's house, my mother was losing her patience.

"You had to invite the whole world, didn't you? We wait for weeks to get this chance to go to the beach, only to sit in the truck all day."

My father did not have a good answer, so he remained silent.

Although it was now past eleven o'clock, Fritz was not ready.

My mother got out of the truck and stood under Fritz's balcony. She looked up and shouted his name.

He came out on the balcony, holding a razor blade, with shaving cream covering half of his face.

"Yes, darling."

"Don't darling me," my mother fumed. "You are holding us up."

"Be there in one minute," he said, "don't fret."

My mother stalked back to the truck, got in and slammed the door.

"I can't stand this German Jew," she said.

We finally had our full complement of passengers, and headed for the road to the beach.

"Stop the truck!" my mother suddenly shouted.

"What's the matter?" my father looked around.

She pointed down the street.

"I see Aryeh and Ahuvah Abend. They are carrying beach bags. You have to give them a lift."

Aryeh and Ahuvah were my cousins. Their mother died when they were little, and they were being raised by their father, who was a night watchman at the harbor. They had barely enough food to eat. Not to pick them up would certainly be a great sin.

By now the truck was wall to wall people. "Not so bad," my father, who always tried to offset my mother's pessimism by looking on the bright side, said. "At least we can't pick up any more passengers."

As I expected, it was wishful thinking. I knew that by the time we got to the bottom of the hill, near the Egged bus terminal, there would be people waiting on the street corner who had missed their bus to the beach, and the more intrepid ones would find a way to get on the truck.

And so it was. When we got down to the bottom of the hill

36

in low gear, before father could resume his speed, several young men began to climb the side of the truck. Some managed to get on, while others remained perched on the side, with one foot hanging out. Father stopped the truck and got out to reason with them. You are not allowed to ride this way, he explained. I will get a big ticket, which you will have to pay.

Somehow they managed to squeeze their other foot into the truck, causing a human congestion that probably made sardines in a can feel comfortable. The truck was so loaded down it nearly sat on its tires, and it moved with great difficulty towards Bat Galim. Needless to say, by the time we reached the beach it was mid-afternoon, and the sun was beating down mercilessly on our heads. My parents were so exhausted from this ordeal, that the moment they spread the blanket on the sand and stretched out, they both fell asleep. But I didn't mind. My prayer was answered. I was at the beach. Life was worth living after all, if only for an hour or two.

10.

In 1970 the Central Conference of American Rabbis, to which I belong, held its first annual convention in Jerusalem. During one of the sessions we had an unexpected visitor. It was David Ben-Gurion, the architect and founding father of the State of Israel, now in his eighties, retired from politics. He was given the speaker's stand by our guest speaker, Professor Gershom Scholem, the famous authority on Jewish mysticism. Ben-Gurion reminisced about the birth of the state and some of its key problems. He observed that even now, 22 years after Israel was started, it was not yet a fully developed state, but only a state in the making.

I suppose that even now, as of this writing, 22 years after Ben-Gurion gave us that impromptu speech, the state is not yet fully formed. But as I look back to the beginning, I can safely say that it took about six months for Israel to be born. The birth started on November 29, 1947, the night the UN took its vote. It was completed on Friday night, May 14, 1948, when Ben-Gurion gathered the leaders of the Yishuv at the old museum in Tel Aviv and proclaimed the establishment of a Jewish state in the land of Israel, to be known as the State of Israel. To paraphrase Dickens, that six-month period was the best and the worst of times. When I consult the history books, I am told that by the time Ben-Gurion was reading the Proclamation of Independence at that museum, things looked quite grim on the ground, and many friends of Israel, including U.S. Secretary of State Marshall, advised B.G. to hold off. It is now agreed that the proclamation made on that day was an act of incredible courage. It was a huge gamble, given the dire conditions of the Yishuv at the time.

How was an eight-year-old to cope at a time like this? For

one thing, I turned to writing poetry. I wrote very patriotic little poems in a little hard bound notebook which I still have, after all these years. I wrote mainly about the determination of the people around me to sacrifice everything in the face of all odds and win. One such poem was read by my proud parents to all their friends and neighbors and was discussed for a long time. It was about the 35 young guerrilla fighters who were sent to the besieged Etzion Bloc outside Jerusalem with arms and ammunition to save the doomed settlers. Before reaching the place they found themselves surrounded by thousands of Arabs and fought to the last man. It was the first serious defeat we Jews suffered in that armed conflict. Those 35, as the thousands who followed them in that war, were the cream of our youth, the best and the brightest. Everyone considered it a personal loss, which I, as a child, must have sensed. I read in the paper that the 35 belonged to the Palmach, a word I did not know at the time. That same afternoon I visited my friend Nir's house, and I saw a black framed picture of Nir's brother on the wall, with a black ribbon hanging down from it. Nir's mother was wearing a black dress and her eyes were swollen from crying.

Nir explained to me his brother had belonged to the Palmach. It was a contraction of two words, *Plugot Mahatz*, meaning Shock Squads. They were the commando force of the Haganah, and they had started to take the lead in the fight for independence. Nir's brother was traveling in a patrol jeep near the Sea of Galilee, guarding the kibbutzim in the area, when the jeep hit a mine and Nir's brother was killed on the spot.

It was then that I sat down to write those little poems, about the 35, about Nir's brother, and about a persecuted little nation called the Jews, who after many years of oppression had vowed not to be passive any longer, and fight to survive and prevail.

11.

Actually the state of Israel was born long before November 29, 1947. That extremely good looking journalist from Vienna, Dr. Theodor Herzl, said in 1897, exactly 50 years before the UN vote, "In Basel I founded the Jewish state. It will become a reality if not in five years, then certainly in fifty." He had organized the Zionist movement and held the Zionist Congress in Basel, Switzerland. The idea was so powerful that it impelled some young men like David Ben-Gurion to go to the wilderness and start the job, while others, like Jabotinsky, started organizing the Jews in Europe, and a chemist named Dr. Chaim Weizmann would start his lobbying efforts in London which would culminate in securing the Balfour Declaration from His Majesty's Government.

But the idea had to transform more than a handful of leaders. It had to reach a critical mass of thousands of people willing to turn it into a living organism that keeps growing until it becomes strong enough to become a new nation. That critical mass was reached in Eastern Europe, particularly in what was and partially still is a country called Poland. The State of Israel was actually born in Poland in the early decades of the twentieth century (one might say, perhaps, Greater Poland, to include areas like Lithuania and parts of the Ukraine).

In Poland prior to the black plague of Naziism lived a Jewish people that spoke Hebrew as well as Yiddish, that had all the Zionist political parties which became reincarnated in Israel, that had Jewish soccer teams, communal organizations, nearly everything a Jewish state can have, except for one thing -- an army. The Jews in Poland, while living in that country in body, did not live there in spirit. Whether secular Zionists or devout religious anti-Zionists, their hearts and souls were in the land of

40

Israel. When the Germans and their Polish, Lithuanian and Ukrainian lackeys massacred three million Polish Jews, they deprived the future State of Israel of a major share of its potential population. That the State of Israel became a reality in spite of this genocide, is no small miracle.

My parents and their friends came from Poland. After the Catastrophe they never wanted to go back, although they had several opportunities to do so. I was never there either, and have no desire to go. But even as an infant I imbibed the spirit of Poland in my mother's milk and my father's stories. After all, my ancestors lived there for centuries, and it was there that the rich lore of my Jewish past was nurtured. Later on, when I studied the history of Poland in high school, I found out that the Polish and the Jewish people in many ways shared a common fate. Poland knew very short periods of independence in recent centuries. Most of the time its people were oppressed by their powerful neighbors, the Germans, the Russians, and others. In World War Two three million Poles were massacred by the Germans, equal to the number of the martyred Polish Jews.

Personally, I bear no grudge against the Poles. They certainly had more than their fair share of trouble. I wouldn't drag them into this story, except for one thing: this is a journey back to the birth of a nation which, in effect, started in Poland. Jewish Poland is no more. But it was in the cities (beginning with the capital, Warsaw, which was the Jerusalem of Europe), towns, villages and hamlets of Poland that the Jewish nation was reborn. Villages like Uvnov, where my mother was born, and Khiruv, from where my father hailed. Even as a child I tried to imagine those places, those quintessential havens of the Jewish soul, the old home, the place of dreams and legends, a world now existing only in books and in the memory of the few who are still alive.

41

My mother hated her native village to the day she died. She could not forgive her father and the rest of the Jews she had left behind for staying there and courting their doom. If a seventeen-year-old girl without a penny to her name could get away, why couldn't they? Not so my father. He only spoke of his village with nostalgia. Intellectually he agreed with my mother, but emotionally he kept dreaming of his village all his life, particularly of his mother, famous for her beauty and kindness. I suppose he passed some of that nostalgia on to me. It was a nostalgia for the people who were lost in the Great Catastrophe, and for their traditions and beliefs. While my father became a secular Zionist like the rest of his friends, unlike most of them he did not turn his back completely on tradition and faith. Personally, he did not have any special relationship with the God of his fathers, but neither did he reject that God. To him, God was still there, where he had left Him, in that little village in Poland. And somehow he must have passed this belief on to me. In a way, I still believe God remained in Poland, and, who knows, God may have gone to Auschwitz with His loyal Jews, while the heretics, like my parents, no longer willing to wait patiently for the messiah, went to the Promised Land. Yes, I know. We would rather believe God lives where He always did, in Zion. Perhaps some day we will find out.

12.

The people who gave birth to the new state in 1948 were young. There were hardly any old people in Haifa in those days. Twenty years earlier, Haifa was a sleepy little town hardly anyone had ever heard of. After the British pushed the Turks out of this part of the Middle East in 1917, they decided to build a major harbor in Haifa, and in the twenties the plan became a reality. The harbor changed the character of the town. It attracted growing numbers of young Jewish pioneers who built roads and all the other infrastructure for what was becoming known as the City of the Future, and started the new town between the Arab string of neighborhoods along the shore and the peaks of Mount Carmel, known as Hadar Ha'Carmel, or the Splendor of Carmel.

By 1948 the older newcomers were in their forties, while the majority were still in their twenties and thirties. I was born into this young community of hardy pioneers who arrived mostly from Poland, pale and thin, and before long became bronzed by the Mediterranean sun and saw their muscles grow and bulge in a way unknown among Jews back in the old country.

It is interesting to note that Ben-Gurion's nickname at the time was *Hazaken,* the Old Man. He was 62 years old.

The Arabs and the British in Haifa in those days were not too old either. The British were mostly military personnel, ranging in age from their twenties to their forties. The Arabs were for the most part young men looking for work, who came from the villages in the Galilee and from as far away as Syria and Lebanon. And then, after the birth of the state, came the Jewish survivors from Europe. They too for the most part were young. Hardly any of the older folks survived.

It was a very youthful environment, which was quite appropriate, since it is usually the young who give birth (not counting our Mother Sarah), and, in effect, we were all giving birth.

Even now, nearly half a century later, a visitor to Israel still gets the feeling it is a country of youth, regardless of the age of any particular individual. That youthful spirit, which is still there, was born during those early years of my childhood.

Which, by the way, was another reason why, despite all the strife and the hardships, it was a wonderful time during which to grow up, a time full of raw energy and wonder and adventure.

And Haifa was, and will always be, one of the most beautiful cities in the world. From the green pine forests on top of Mount Carmel to the blue bay and the shoreline stretching as far as Lebanon, it is a city of a thousand sights, rivaling one another in sheer beauty. In Europe they used to say, "To see Naples and to die." They might as well have said it about Haifa.

Yes, I know. The most beautiful city in the world is Jerusalem. No two ways about it. The Talmud says, "Ten measures of beauty came into the world, and Jerusalem took nine." Jerusalem's beauty is more than physical. For lack of a more tangible word, we'd call it spiritual. Haifa's beauty is just that, the beauty of nature, a gift to the mortals from the gods.

Which is why we all fell in love with her -- Jews, Arabs, British, everyone. And everyone wanted to hold on to it. The British left in 1948 very reluctantly. The Arabs made a stand and fought for it. They only left when they thought the Jews would be driven into the sea by the combined armies of the neighboring Arab countries, and they, the Arabs of Haifa, would be able to come back to occupy two homes each -- their own home and one Jewish home.

13.

Few people dominated my childhood more than a man named Fritz Kalman. Fritz was in charge of the fish section in the Tnuvah food cooperative in Haifa. In this capacity he was responsible for contracting my father's services to transport the fish from the Haifa harbor to the main distribution centers around the country. In many ways Fritz embodied the spirit of Israel in those days. He was reckless, witty, adventurous, totally dedicated to his pioneering mission, a loyal friend, a great swimmer, and a wit.

He and my parents and the rest of their generation were -- on the surface -- ordinary people. Most of them did not get a chance to finish high school. They worked as common laborers in Palestine of the 20s and 30s, doing whatever work they could find. But there was nothing ordinary about them. They were the brave few who left Europe in time, before the German Beast was unleashed on Europe and the world. One from a family, two or three from a village, a handful from a town. Those were the hardy souls who saw what was coming, and did not choose to live in a fool's paradise, as did the rest of their fellow-Jews. From their generations' long Jewish tradition in Europe they derived spiritual strength and moral values, shedding off the ritual minutiae and the host of superstitions which encrusted the Jewish religion in early 20th century Europe. From the teaching of Hebrew poets like Bialik and Tchernichovsky and Zionist leaders like Herzl, Jabotinsky and Ben-Gurion they derived the vision of a Jewish national home and a rebirth of Jewish military prowess, creative genius, and an advanced techno-scientific society. All those things that lay dormant for centuries came back to life, like a body existing in suspended animation stirred from its long sleep. It was a miracle of rare device, a resurrection of a people. The dry bones of the long diaspora grew skin and sinews and stood up and started to march. One from a family and two from a town they marched together to the land of Israel, crossing borders and seas, and the process started. A collective will was set in motion, and nothing could stop it.

Fritz was one of the founders of the Jewish fishing industry in the new state of Israel. Back in antiquity there were Jewish fishermen. Among the tribes of Israel, Zebulun was known to specialize in fishing. In the time of Jesus, there were Jewish fishermen in the Sea of Galilee. But for the past two thousand years one would be hard put to find Jewish fishermen. All this changed when Fritz and his friends started Kibbutz Ein Gev on the eastern bank of the Sea of Galilee, and renewed Jewish fishing in that romantic body of water. From there, Fritz moved to Haifa, where he took part in establishing sea fishing in the Mediterranean Sea, including deep sea fishing. Later he would take part in starting the fishing industry in Eilat, on the Red Sea, and in the late fifties and sixties he would become involved in sending fishing vessels to the Horn of Africa and other far-flung places.

On a recent trip to Israel I looked him up, not having seen him for nearly forty years. At eighty-two, Fritz still had his wits about him, and has remained the same wonderful conversationalist he was in his younger days. He reminisced about Ein Gev in the thirties, when he and his fellow kibbutzniks were trying to find a way to get along with the Arab fishermen in the Sea of Galilee, and about his role in the battle for Haifa in 1948, which is recounted elsewhere in this book. He took me back to my childhood, and it occurred to me that there was so much going on in those days to which I, as a child, was not privy. Everything in which my father and he and the rest of those men

46

at the food cooperative were involved was always shrouded in a veil of mystery, and I wondered for years what went on.

Fritz smiled. The same old mischievous smile I remembered so well.

"Much of our life in those days was clandestine. We were building a country under the noses of the British and the Arabs, and practically everything we did was illegal. We had to be extremely cautious, hard working, resourceful, and inventive."

I pressed him for more details. He went on to explain that the entire Jewish male population of Haifa, from age eighteen to fifty, was organized in a local defense system, except for a few who preferred to belong to the more radical Irgun. People were responsible for the defense of their own neighborhoods, and many, like him and my father, did guard duty at night, with or without a concealed firearm. Weapons, mostly antiquated low quality ones, were hidden in many points in the city. The main labor union of the Yishuv, or Histadrut, sponsored the Haganah organization, through its construction section, the Solel Boneh. Haifa was the stronghold of the Haganah in Israel, since it was a city of laborers, most of them rugged people. The other stronghold were the kibbutzim, the communal farms, where a new breed of Jewish farmers learned how to farm and physically defend their settlements. Tel Aviv and Jerusalem were more bourgeois, middle class cities, but even there the Haganah was quite active and had a large membership.

Fritz and my father belonged to different units of the Haganah in Haifa. But in one area they used to collaborate from time to time. They both took advantage of their special status in Haifa harbor, where Fritz operated cold storage for the fish harvest, and where my father drove his truck almost every day to pick up the fish crates from the warehouse. Every once in a while a shipment of illegal weapons arrived at Haifa harbor on some Greek, or Italian, or Turkish ship. Fritz arranged for the precious cargo to be transferred in the middle of the night several miles offshore to one of the fishing boats. The fishermen would hide the weapons inside fish crates, which were then loaded on my father's truck. Fritz would get into the truck's cab and ride with my father to the main gate of the harbor, where the British guards inspected every vehicle. He knew the guards, and had some choice fish ready for them. This would make them lose interest in inspecting the truck, and they would wave it on. The weapons were transferred to hiding places in Haifa, known as "sliks," and became part of the Haganah's arsenal.

This was a routine activity, Fritz recalls. But some of the things they did were not routine at all. One of the activities which required constant inventiveness and improvisation was bringing illegal immigrants to the shores of the promised land, one of the major tasks of the Yishuv during almost the entire period of the British Mandate, particularly after Hitler's rise to power in Germany. The history of the illegal Jewish immigrations to Palestine is one of the most stirring chapters in all of Jewish history, the stuff biblical stories are made of. Fritz was right there in the middle of it all, and the way he reminisces about it, some sixty years later, makes it clear to me it was the most dramatic time of his life.

In the thirties, illegal immigration intensified, and Jewish fishermen and seamen were approached by the Haganah to lend a helping hand. Fritz and his fellow fishermen from Ein Gev took time out from their work at the fishing kibbutz and went to Jaffa and to other points on the Mediterranean shore to help bring the "illegals" to a safe haven. The immigrants sailed on small vessels, the size of large yachts, from ports in the Balkan countries. They would arrive at night, with their lights off, to dodge the searching eyes of the British navy, and stop at about half a mile distance from the shore, at an agreed upon point. Fritz and his men would swim to the boat, lower down the life boats, and load them with immigrants. The entire operation had to be accomplished swiftly and quietly, to escape British patrols, who would send the immigrants back to Europe or to one of their remote colonies. Anyone who is familiar with navigation or sea-related activities knows that bad weather is the enemy of the navigator, and sailing plans are often subject to change. Here, however, there was no room for change. The human cargo had to be unloaded in the middle of a storm, in driving rain, in bitter cold. Once on shore, the "illegals" had to be taken away to some Jewish farms or towns in the area, where they were issued documentation and dispersed in local Jewish communities. Each time a shipload arrived, Fritz recalls, some new problems arose, and new solutions had to be found.

One time a boat arrived offshore in the north, in Shavey Tzion, near Nahariah, with some two hundred immigrants. By the time Fritz and his kibbutzniks arrived on the scene, the British had imposed one of their frequent curfews on the Western Galilee area, which meant that no one was allowed to leave his home or travel on the roads. Here they were, with two hundred newly arrived "illegals," not able to go anywhere.

The commander of the operation was not about to give up. He quickly came up with a plan: it so happened that a road was being built at the time between the moshav, or farming community of Shavey Tzion and the coast. The commander got in touch with the moshav and explained the problem. He told the engineer in charge of the project he needed the uniforms and the equipment of the road construction crew, which were quickly sent over to him. The newly arrived immigrants, hardly knowing what was happening to them, were dressed in the road builders' clothes and were told to carry the hoes, sledge hammers, spades and picks. Next their faces were duly smeared with tar and dirt, to make it look as though they had just spent a hard day of work on the asphalt. Next the Haganah commander contacted British police headquarters in Haifa and explained his problem. He was in charge of a road construction project, and he had two hundred construction workers who were stuck on the shore near Nahariah, and could not get back home to Haifa. Could the British arrange safe passage for them?

The British were happy to oblige. They sent over army trucks and armor and transported all two hundred "illegals," for whom they had been looking high and low, back to the safety of their "homes" in Haifa. The Haganah arranged home hospitality for the entire group, and the next day they were sent under the unsuspecting noses of the British police to settlements on the coast and in the Valley of Jezreel.

On another occasion, a group of "illegals" was taken to shore north of Acre, when the word came that the British police were on their way, and there may not be enough time to whisk the newly arrived to safety. Here again the Haganah came up with a last minute solution. Some attractive female members of the Haganah were sent over, dressed as ladies of the night. They stopped the British convoy a mile or two down the road from the disembarkation point, and kept them busy for a couple of hours. By that time all the immigrants were taken away to a safe place.

But things did not always work out so smoothly. One time a large number of immigrants reached the shore of Tel Aviv. The Haganah came up with a plan to organize a large demonstration on the shore protesting British restrictions against the Yishuv, so as to keep the British police busy and to use the confusion of the demonstration to bring the immigrants to shore. This time the plan was foiled by an informer who tipped off the British, who quickly dispatched their frigates and fired on the ship, forcing it to go back.

When World War Two started, illegal immigration dwindled to a trickle. It became nearly impossible to find boats or seamen who were willing to risk their lives under war conditions. Fritz and his friends went back to fishing. He, my father, and the rest of the Yishuv experienced a tremendous sense of frustration not being able to do anything to help their brothers and sisters in Europe. All they could do now was hope and pray the Germans and their allies would soon be defeated, and they would all be able to see their loved ones once again. It was not meant to be.

By the time I came on the scene, clandestinity had become a way of life with people like Fritz and my father. On the surface, they led very ordinary lives, operating the fish section of the national food cooperative. But they were all biding their time as they prepared for the great moment when at long last a state would be born, and all their clandestinity, all their countless covert adventures would be put to the final test of bringing that state into life and making it last.

Then came 1948 and the War of Independence. The men at Tnuvah were now in their late thirties, too old to become combat soldiers. Of the entire gang -- Fritz, Yoskeh, Naftali, Moishe and Zvi, the only one who was drafted into active duty was my father, Zvi, mainly because of his truck, which was vital for the war effort. The rest remained in the market and in the harbor, where they carried on with the fish business. Fritz, recalling those days, tells me that he did make an effort to be drafted. This was after he was wounded in the battle of Haifa. The foot wound was not serious, and it quickly healed. But he had a much more serious problem with his back, which went back to the days when he used to swim out to the ships to bring the "illegals" to shore. When he enlisted after the battle of Haifa, he was sent on training, and had to carry a heavy machine gun. His back snapped, and they had to carry him back to base on a stretcher. He was given a special certificate and sent back to Tnuvah, to take charge of the fish department. "I was very disappointed," the octogenarian sighs. "I wanted so badly to extend my youth by serving in the new army. But it was not meant to be."

They all wanted to extend their youth. They were a generation of young idealistic starry-eyed men and women who never grew old, not even at eighty.

14.

One of the problems facing the Jewish fishermen in those days was nomenclature. The Hebrew language did not have words for parts of boats and different kinds of fish and all the sailing and fishing terminology which is so well developed in a language like English. In fact, fishing was by no means the only field suffering from this problem. It was a rather pervasive problem.

One of my early recollections is the time my father took me on a stroll in Gan Binyamin, or Benjamin Park, not far from our home on Luntz Street. He was very interested in finding out the names of the trees and the flowers in the park. He always dreamed of the big forests back home in Poland, and, like all Zionists, trees held a special place in his heart. In those days the Hebrew language was being revived, and most trees and flowers had yet to be given names. I took great pride in the fact my father was asking little me for such important information, and since I was not able to name trees other than pine, cypress or eucalyptus, or flowers other than roses, poppies or cyclamens, I started making up names. It was not a very honest thing to do, but unbeknownst to me I was taking part in the process of creating the new Hebrew, and I had just as much right to make up new names as anyone else. Most important, I made my unsuspecting father happy. He was proud of me, and was happy to know my teachers were doing such as good job with me. He did not remember those names of flowers and trees anyway, so it didn't really matter. A tree remained a tree and a flower remained a flower.

I am not trying to belittle my father. Far from it. He spoke Polish, Ukrainian, German, Yiddish and Arabic in addition to Hebrew. It was not his fault those words were yet to be invented, or that the ones that were already in place were not part of his daily vocabulary. Learning all those words was a luxury he could not afford. He worked 12 to 14 hours every day, and most nights he had guard duty. His hope was that my life would be more normal and enlightened than his.

And because he was gone most of the time, on those rare occasions when he did find the time to take a walk with me in the park I was very happy. Having him all to myself was a rare treat, which I cherished and treasured. I must admit, I did feel guilty making up those words, but I just couldn't bring myself to sound ignorant and disappoint him. And, to this day, I really wonder whether he knew all along I was making them up, just to make him proud of me, and yet chose to condone my behavior.

15.

Our lives were full of anomalies. Very few of us had extended families, and so we formed surrogate families, made up of friends of our fathers and mothers from the Old Country, and the children of those friends. We were about four or five families in Haifa at that time, including my own, that formed one of those surrogate extended families. There were Dov and Lola Freund. Dov was my father's childhood friend from Poland. Lola had met Dov through my father, and I think my father always had a warm spot in his heart for Lola. Then there were Shlomo and Shanka, or Yafah (same name, first in Polish and the second in Hebrew) Silberman, also friends from the old country. Then there was Fela, who lost her husband when I was too young to remember, and drifted out of the group. Finally there was another couple who was more peripheral to the group, and I have forgotten their names.

The three hard core couples in this surrogate family were my parents, the Freunds, and the Silbermans. The Silbermans had two sons, the oldest of whom was Michael, who was two years older than I. The Freunds had one son, named Donny, two years younger than I. I did not have any brothers, so in a way Michael became my older brother, and Donny my younger brother.

I lost track of Michael, or Micha, as we called him in those days, early in my teens. When I was six and he was eight we were good friends, and he used to teach me the facts of life, particularly those facts which parents would not tell children about in those days (although our parents -- under the influence of Marxism -- practiced free love before we were born, they were great prudes when it came to telling children the facts of life. It seems that in raising children they were just as prudish as their parents back home in Poland, who lived in a very strict religious

55

environment. This too was one of the great anomalies we grew up with). For this I was very grateful to him. He must have been the first boy who taught me how to stimulate my sexual fantasies. But by the time I was thirteen or fourteen he had lost interest in me, and to this day anything I know about his life is second hand, and not much of it is complimentary.

Donny, on the other hand, has been a lifelong friend. Though we are now middle aged men, with grownup children, living continents apart, our early childhood friendship has survived years of separation, and has remained strong. The bond between us has lasted from those early Haifa days, when Donny, an only child, still looks upon me as his older brother, having passed on to him the facts of life taught to me by Micha, and played with him, rode bikes with him, wrestled with him, bragged to him about my imagined sexual exploits, and showed him a good time.

16.

My mother, I was told, made two attempts to leave home and go to the Promised Land. The first failed, but the second succeeded. She was not quite eighteen when she made the first attempt. Apparently, her father was dead set against her leaving home and joining those godless Zionists who were breaking the laws of the Torah in those secular settlements in the Holy Land. The idea of making aliyah came to her in her early teens. She could not tolerate the thought of living in a country where she would always be a second class citizen, and she had no use for the rigid religious life around her. She and her father were always arguing about these matters, but my grandfather, bless his soul, never gave up hope to bring his wayward daughter to the straight and narrow.

Before she turned eighteen she decided to leave home secretly, in the middle of the night, without telling anybody. She got up after everyone had fallen asleep, got dressed, and went to the train station. After she left the house her father must have sensed something, and went to check her room. He realized what had happened, and got dressed quickly and went to wake up Moishe, the wagon driver, who lived next door. He paid him extra to drive to the next town as fast as his old nags could possibly pull the wagon. They arrived at the train station in the next town an hour later. My grandfather knew that my mother had to change trains in that town, and that usually it took two or three hours. So if he hurried up he had a chance of catching up with her.

His plan worked out. There she was, sitting in the train station, bundled in her shawl, her teeth chattering because of the cold winter night.

he told her she should be ashamed of herself, pulled her by

the arm, and dragged her to the wagon. She did not put up too much resistance, and went along, without saying a word.

From that day on all she could think of was how to find a way to make aliyah with her father's approval. The answer came one day in the form of a family friend, called Reb Dov Beirish Ortner. Ortner was a printer, who had decided to settle in the Land of Israel. He was a well-to-do man, and had no trouble obtaining a Certificate from the British Government. Ortner was a good friend of my grandfather's, and he heard about my mother's burning desire to live in the Land of Israel. One day he turned to my grandfather and told him,

"Reb Naftoli, you have nothing to worry about your daughter, Haykeh, may she be healthy and strong. I will look after her personally, and everything will be all right. You can let her go without a second thought."

My grandfather finally relented, and gave my mother his blessing. She joined a group of the Zionist Youth and took the train to Constanta, on the Black Sea shore of Romania, where she boarded the ship to Palestine.

Once there, she hardly ever saw her sponsor, Reb Ortner, who lived in Tel Aviv, while she lived in the north, in Haifa. Ortner remained a religious Jew all his life, and one of his sons became a rabbi. He made several attempts to bring my mother back into the fold, but she had a different, non-religious agenda. She remained grateful to him for the rest of her life, but while he remained within the Orthodox community, she became a secular Zionist.

And so my mother embarked on her life's mission, to create something out of nothing, to build a homeland out of sand and rocks and against great adversity. And she did.

58

17.

One thing people like my mother, or leaders like Ben-Gurion and all the others, including Abraham Stern-Yair, or Golda Meir, or the founder of my school, Dr. Biram, must have understood early on about life in this new land, namely, that the undertaking was enormous, and only through extreme self-discipline, a willingness to adhere to very rigid rules, and constant self-sacrifice, would this dream have a chance of becoming a reality. And so we became a society living by very strict norms, which were not always pleasant or comfortable, and which not everyone seemed able to tolerate. I learned later on that of all the people who came to live in the Land of Israel in the twentieth century, only a minority remained. This does not surprise me. It took an unusual breed of people to create the state. People with great physical stamina, deep conviction, great persistence, courage, and an understanding of what it was all about.

These people also had glaring faults and shortcomings, but they were true pioneers, nation-builders, people of destiny. They were not always the most congenial people to be around, but you knew you could rely on them, they wouldn't let you down. They were people like Fritz, and my mother, and my father, and all the rest, rugged individuals who at the same time were team players and highly disciplined soldiers. Without them, no leader, no matter how brilliant or persuasive, could have ever pulled off that miracle. Each one of them made his or her own contribution to the general effort, some more than others, but all in good measure, and out of the sum total of their lives came something unlike anything we have ever known. It was a moment in time when people rose above the level of the everyday and reached a higher level, a higher rung, as the Hasidim would say, and showed the world how human beings can reach for the stars, and bring them down to earth.

No, it was not an ideal life by any means. Certainly not for me and my loved ones. But it was an honor and a privilege to be part of that life. It is not granted to humans too often in the course of recorded time.

18.

I was never taught to hate the Arabs. They were not the enemy. Their interests and ours were at odds, which produced conflicts. But the enemy was foreign rule, and antisemitism, and all the forces that oppressed not only Jews but people in general. I wish things had turned out differently in 1948. If people really knew how to get along with one another -- which unfortunately they do not -- things would have been quite different. If the Arabs back in 1948, instead of being led by a hate-monger like Haj Amin Al-Husseini, the Grand Mufti of Jerusalem, had been led by some truly enlightened leader, someone comparable to the late Anwar Sadat, things might have turned out differently. Sadat might have said, Okay, let's sit down and talk. Really (I love the way he used to pronounce the word "really," rolling his r), there is a vast Middle East with room for everyone. The UN Decision is a historical imperative which we all must learn how to live with. Both Jews and Arabs have lived in the Middle East since time immemorial, and now finally the world is offering independence to both of us. Isn't it wonderful? For centuries, the Arabs of the Middle East were severely oppressed by a Muslim ruler called the Ottoman Empire, or the Turks. It was one of the worst foreign rules in human history. It left us Arabs poor, ignorant, conflicted, and divided. At the same time, Jews were persecuted in Europe, and finally decimated. Now both Jews and Arabs have an opportunity to begin a Golden Age, not unlike the one they had ten centuries ago, in Muslim Spain, before the Crusaders turned on the Arabs and the Spanish Inquisition on the Jews.

History, of course, is not a matter of "what if," but "what is." And what was in 1948 and is now, at the end of the century, is continued conflict. Jews and Arabs in the Middle East have now fought several wars, the most recent indirectly, namely, the

Gulf War, which saw Iraq fire Scud missiles on Tel Aviv and on Haifa. But as a native of Haifa, when I see an Arab I do not see an enemy. As a child I played with Arab children, as a teenager I went to school with them, I studied their language and culture, and, culturally, we Jews are related to them, not only because the Bible says so, but because there is no food in the world I like better (as do most Israelis) than Arab food, because my language and theirs come from the same root, and because we both hail from the same corner of the world.

I still remember the days prior to the 47 vote and the 48 war, my earliest childhood, when my mother and other housewives on our street bartered with Arab peddlers from nearby villages, who exchanged rice for brown sugar. The Arabs learned how to chat in Yiddish, and the housewives picked up a fair amount of Arabic conversation, and each side benefited from the offerings of the other side. I used to visit an Arab boy my age down the street from us, and his mother would give me a slice of rye bread on which she put oil and salt, a custom I had never seen before or since, except that a few months ago in San Francisco I saw it again at a rather elegant Italian restaurant not far from Fisherman's Wharf.

Much to my regret, many of the Arabs I knew in those days became refugees, and more than a few filled the ranks of the PLO. If I were an Arab from Haifa, I would probably have done the same thing. And for all these years the debate has been raging around the world, did we Jews chase the Arabs out of Haifa, or did they leave on their own? It was really a combination of both. The Arabs started the war, and the Jews fought back. But the Haganah did make attempts to persuade the Arab population to stay. Makeshift armored cars with loudspeakers circulated in the Arab neighborhoods and made their plea. But the Arabs listened to the Mufti, and also to their own fears. Many of them were intent on, to use their expression, *atbakh al yahud*, kill the Jews, and so they were convinced the Jews would do the same to them. *Honi soit qui mal y pense.* Now, years later, many of them wish they had stayed.

19.

The best way to describe life in Haifa during the months prior to the UN vote and for the entire year that followed, is by using the expression "days and nights of fire." The fire came in many shapes and forms, from all sides. The two outlawed underground organizations, the Irgun and the Lehi, actually started their war of liberation long before the official war that followed Ben-Gurion's proclamation of the new state in May 1948. Perhaps the greatest fire during that period was the one that was started at the oil refineries in Haifa Bay, in 1947. I had just turned eight, and I remember a bright sunny day, as I was standing on the corner of Luntz and Sokolov, in front of my house. It was the middle of the day, and all of a sudden day turned into night. We heard some distant explosions, and a huge black cloud of smoke rose up in the sky and covered the sun. It was a sudden and total eclipse. I rushed home, afraid to stay outside, and asked my mother what happened.

Much to my surprise, my mother was beaming.

"It's very good," she said.

"What's very good?" I asked.

"They did it."

"Who?"

"They blew up the refineries."

She held me in her arms and clutched me against her bosom.

"Those boys," she whispered, "with boys like these I know we will win, we must, no question about it."

Her irrational joy reassured me. Soon the dark smoke began to disperse and it was sunny and bright once again. Even as a child I understood the message. Jews were sending a signal to the world. We are no cowards. We can fight, and we can win. The war of liberation had begun.

Even as I child I was awed by those mysterious young men who did those hair raising things. My friends and their families were not supporters of the *porshim*, or Separatists, as they were known in those days. Haifa was a town of mainstream, labor Zionist Jews, who took their cues from Mr. Ben-Gurion, the archenemy of the Separatists, who, as the official head of the Yishuv, had to apologize for their actions to the British authorities time and again. The leader of the Lehi, Avraham Stern, known by his *nom de guerre* as Yair, had been killed by the British back in 1942, and it was not quite clear who their new leader was. The Irgun was headed by a mystery man named Begin, whom no one ever saw, but there were always rumors circulating about his whereabouts. The British searched everywhere for him, but could never find him. He ran the entire Irgun from some unknown hiding place somewhere in the country, and remained completely elusive.

Once my father took me in his truck on one of his fish delivery trips to Tel Aviv. Along came one of his young assistants, a Sephardic Jew name Elie. On the way back from Tel Aviv that evening Elie and I rode on the back of the truck. We got around to talking about the blowing up of the refineries. Elie put his arms around me and hugged me, kissing me on my head.

"I'm going to tell you a secret which you must never repeat," he said. "You promise?"

I promised.

"I am a member of the Irgun."

My reaction was one of total incredulity. Never before did I hear an adult make such a statement. For anyone to admit openly in those days to being a member of the Irgun meant arrest, torture, and a possible death sentence. I felt I had just been admitted into the most important secret society in the world. I was so excited I could hardly fall asleep that night.

One day I came home from school and I stood on the balcony of our neighbors' apartment on the third floor, watching the goings on in the street below. It was an ordinary afternoon, if indeed there were any ordinary afternoons in those days. It was a very tense time. A few days before a boat carrying illegal immigrants, in other words, Holocaust survivors from Europe, had arrived in Haifa harbor, and there was a clash between the immigrants and the British police. Two survivors were killed by British police fire and several wounded.

I could see the entire neighborhood from that balcony -- Luntz Street down below, Sokolov running uphill to the left, the beginning of Sirkin to the right. In front of me was a wide open field where my father used to park his truck, and where I often played with my friends. I saw two young men across the street on that field looking for something. They soon left, and the street was going about its usual business. Down below there was a poultry shop, full of cages with live turkeys. It was the week before Purim, and one of my friends had told me that if you yelled "Today is Purim," the turkeys would yell back the same words. I had tried it once or twice that day on my way home from school, and indeed the turkeys greeted me with a chorus that sounded quite close to what I said. Then again, I did not shout anything else, which might have disproved the theory.

In any case, I was standing on that balcony in late afternoon as the sun began to tip the horizon, when a British jeep with four soldiers came down Sokolov Street and turned left on Luntz, where I was standing. The soldiers were wearing red berets, which meant they were paratroopers. We called them *kalaniyot*, the Hebrew word for red poppy flowers, which grow on Mount

66

Carmel during the winter. The jeep was passing under the balcony when suddenly an explosion was heard in the street and the jeep went up in the air and landed on its side on the edge of the field across the street. People on the street below stopped to look. When the smoke and dust cleared up I saw one of the soldiers climb out of the jeep. He was covered with dust and was bleeding from a cut on his cheek. He strutted to the middle of the street, took out his pistol, and, holding it aloft, stopped the traffic on the intersection of Sokolov and Luntz. I did not see any of the other three soldiers come out. Soon a military ambulance arrived on the scene, at which point my mother came in and took me downstairs to our apartment.

That evening the British announced an overnight curfew in our part of town. No one was to leave his house after seven o'clock in the evening. Around seven we were sitting in the kitchen eating supper, when we heard a knock on the door, and two armed soldiers came in and told us they had orders to search the apartment. They looked through our closets and found an amusement park type air gun, a present from a relative from America who had visited us a month earlier. It was a toy rifle which could hardly hurt a fly. You cocked it by opening and closing it where the barrel met the butt, and by loading it with either soft lead pellets or small darts. One soldier brought the small rifle into the kitchen and asked my father what it was for.

My father pointed at me and smiled.

"The boy," he said.

The Englishman turned the gun, pointing it to the floor, and handed it to me.

"Sorry to disturb your dinner," he said, and they walked out.

The next day we learned that the mine that blew up the jeep was wired to some device found in the house next door to us. All the residents of that house were ordered to pack their belongings and move to an empty schoolhouse in a different part of town. We organized a neighborhood relief mission and went there every day for two weeks to bring them food and other necessities, and help them through their period of exile.

Fires, bombs, explosions, curfews, searches were nearly a daily routine in Haifa in 1946 and 1947. Looking back, those were the birth pangs of the new state. But it was nothing compared to the birth itself, which, as I mentioned, lasted for about six months, from November 47 to April 48, culminating in those two days of nonstop fighting during Passover, when Haifa finally became an integral part of the fledgling state. During that time I celebrated my ninth birthday, and I saw a nation being born.

20.

Life, death, birth, creation. All human existence revolves around these polarities. But most people throughout time experience them in manageable, fairly predictable portions. Not so during my childhood. As a child I stood at the end of one world and on the threshold of another. I saw worlds disappear and new ones being created. I was born a British subject in the historical land of the Jews to parents who were Polish citizens. At nine I became an Israeli citizen. Later on I would find myself in South America and travel to the United States to go to college, using a Uruguayan passport. I would become a U.S. citizen (and hold both Israeli and U.S. citizenships), and would have a daughter born in Guatemala which made her a Guatemalan-Israeli-American citizen. And I am only in my fifties, wondering what in the world will happen next. Still, the most extraordinary time of my life was my early childhood, when I saw Israel being born. In a way it was all so ordinary, coming home that afternoon from the movies, where I saw a mediocre musical called *Fiesta*, starring Esther Williams, to find out that the world agreed to having a Jewish state on the face of this earth. We were all rather ordinary people -- my parents and I, our friends and neighbors, living in an ordinary town called Haifa, which was certainly no Paris or London or Rome. And yet we were part of something greater than ourselves, and we knew it. We were the bricks and mortar, the building blocks of a new nation which was reborn at least twice before during the past thirty-three centuries. There were only half a million of us at that time in the entire country, and now -- half a century later -- there are five millions. In other words, each one of us, in less than two generations, has become ten. And more are coming. And more will.

Which reminds me of one of my favorite Hebrew poems of

that era, by the modest poet Yehuda Karni:

With every rolling stone put me in the breach
And fasten me with a sledgehammer,
Perhaps I may make amends to my land, and atone
for my people's sin, who did not mend the ruins.

How good it is to be a stone among the stones of Jerusalem
How happy I am to be part of the wall.
Why should my body be less than my soul, which, through fire
and flood
Walked with this people, either shouting or still?

Pick me up along with the Jerusalem stone, and put me in the
wall,
And plaster me over,
And from the mighty wall let my bones sing their song
As they yearn for the messiah.

21.

The apartment we lived in on the corner of Luntz and Sokolov was a small two bedroom apartment which we shared with another family. It had a small kitchen, one bathroom (a tub and a sink), a toilet (no tub or shower, only a toilet seat and a small sink), and two small balconies, one for the kitchen and the other for the second bedroom. This was a typical apartment of that period, and some of those features haven't changed to this day, even in the newest Israeli apartments. The house was a three story, six family apartment building, which still stands there to this day. It was built in the early forties of cinderblock, cement and plaster, a rather simple, rudimentary box, painted white on the outside. The only ingenious feature of that typical house were the balconies, which were generously added to three of the four sides of the building -- front, back, and along the side street. In those days we had neither heat nor air conditioning. Summer in the Middle East can be quite suffocating, even in Haifa, which nestles on the side of a mountain and gets some cool sea breeze most of the year. The balcony is typical of tropical and subtropical countries. It allows you to get fresh air or sunshine. It also allows you to be in touch with life outside, on the street, in the yard, on different sides of the house. No wonder we spent a good part of our life on those balconies, keeping cool, keeping in touch, and making sure we did not miss anything. No wonder so many of my more pleasant as well as stirring childhood memories are balcony-based.

In that house I spent my preschool and early school years, till 1948, when the neighborhood became too dangerous, and we had to move away to safer surroundings, up the mountain. It was there I spent part of my infancy in the bomb shelter in the basement, waiting for Mussolini's planes to bomb us. Then, after the war ended, soldiers from the British Army's Jewish Brigade started to arrive in our town. They were penniless and had no place to go. I was about six or seven, and I remember one night two of them came knocking on our door. They asked us if we could put them up for the night -- only one night. My mother would not be easily fooled. She told them we shared the apartment with another family with an infant, which meant that my parents, my two year old sister and I shared the same bedroom, and there no room for another living soul. Reluctantly, they went up to the third floor. We heard loud voices as our neighbors upstairs started arguing with them. I heard one soldier shout,

"We laid down our lives for you, and you can't do us even this small favor."

The couple they were arguing with, I believe their names were Ruja and Peter, did not have any children, and were lucky enough to have a spare room.

Peter was mollified.

"Only one night!," he said menacingly.

I was standing in the stairwell watching the entire drama.

One of the Jewish Brigade soldiers put two fingers in his mouth and let out a thunderous whistle. There was noise downstairs at the street entrance, and up came a third comrade, carrying three mattresses on his back.

"You said two!" Peter roared.

The whistler shrugged his shoulders.

"Only one night," he reminded Peter.

Those three stayed for a month. They had taken over the room, and they hung brown military blankets between their sleeping quarters and the legitimate occupants of the apartment. It took some unusual methods to finally evict them, but this is another story.

My mother, by the way, did not lie when she told the invaders we had another family living in our two bedroom apartment. In those days many families shared apartments. It would usually start with two young, newly married couples, who could make do with almost anything. And then the children started to arrive. First it was me, then my sister, Dahlia, and then the other couple, the Landaus, had their baby. The biggest problem in those apartments were the kitchen and the bathroom. It seemed you always had to wait to get into the bathroom, and it was common practice to raise one's voice when someone seemed to linger inside longer than necessary. But somehow the people got used to waiting for the bathroom. What they never seemed to get used to, particularly the women, was the kitchen. To a woman, a kitchen is her castle, her exclusive domain. Two housewives in one kitchen was like having two queens serve on the same throne. It was constant conflict. No matter how hard the two homemakers tried to work things out, it always came to a head. You took my salt! You stole my egg! You used my pot! And on and on. In those shared kitchens relations between the two housewives ranged from tight lipped toleration to outright warfare.

To me as a little child, this human density was not unpleasant, but rather interesting and reassuring. I did not have any grandparents or uncles and aunts, or any other relatives. We were the children of young pioneers, and having other people sharing our space and our life was a kind of surrogate, undeclared extended family. All this changed as I was getting older. By the time I was reaching puberty I wanted as much privacy as I could get. Fortunately, by then I already lived higher up on the mountain and had my own room.

22.

But in 1947-48 everything was abnormal, and sharing everything, including your own living quarters, with others seemed perfectly natural. The Arabs around the corner also lived in small, crowded quarters. Everywhere you went you always seemed to be tripping over someone as you moved from room to room, from room to balcony, or through the staircase to the street. What is also curious, is the fact that although we lived in small crowded apartments, the furniture and the furnishings in those apartments were bulky and sometimes downright huge, and often left little floor space to get around. Years later they would develop more practical furniture for apartments, both in Israel and around the world, styles like Danish Modern, beds that close against the wall, hidden kitchenettes, and so on. But my parents and their peers, who came from Europe, brought with them the style of big clumsy furniture they had back home -- big mahogany cupboards and closets (with lock and key on each door), dining room tables with big sculpted legs, chairs too heavy to pick up, brass beds, and along with all this -- to complete the picture -- bedding which included goose down quilts which rose one or two feet above the bed (my mother called them *pereneh*), no doubt most suitable for the cold winters in Poland rather than the hot nights of the Middle East.

I can easily go back to December, 1947, and see in my mind's eyes the interior of that apartment during that time. It is early Saturday morning, the day known in Israel as Shabbat. I wake up in the large bed, covered with the huge quilt, my head resting on a large plump pillow filled with the same goose down as the quilt, all part of my parents' patrimony from Poland. There is no school today. I am ecstatic, and I start singing,

Yom zeh m'chubad...
This day is honored above all other days,
For on it the Rock of the Universe rested.

Why my socialist-secularist teacher, Ephratya, taught her class such a traditional song, is not exactly clear. She certainly had no intention of instilling in us any religious fervor. But this morning I find this particular song best suited for the way I feel about my day off (our weekend back then consisted of one day, Saturday). The main reason is that I have a good book to read, and I have been waiting since yesterday for a chance to start reading it. Reading is the greatest passion of my childhood.

I hear a distant explosion, and then there is some machine gun burst nearby and the popping of sniper bullets. I raise the quilt up to my eyeballs. Am I in danger? Of course I am. We all are.

I look at the tall mahogany linen cupboard across the room. It towers like a mountain. Some day I'll be tall enough to reach up to the top without having to stand on a chair. My mother used to hide things on top of the cupboard, but when she found out I could reach that height, she started using more ingenious hiding places. Recently, my mother started playing a game with me. She had gotten me started on collecting stamps from all over the world. I quickly developed a passion for stamps. So she bought a large cellophane-wrapped package with about 1000 stamps of the world, and each time I got a good grade or did something worthwhile she would give me a few. One of my biggest wishes during my growing years was to discover where she hid the package of stamps. I never did. Whenever I came close, she seemed to have sensed it and changed the hiding place. How I failed to find a package practically the size of a shoebox in a two

bedroom apartment during a period of some five or six years is
something I'll never be able to figure out.

Well, I am still in bed, and there is still some sporadic
shooting. My parents are in the kitchen, speaking in Polish.
Whenever they don't want me to understand what they are saying
they revert back to Polish. Normally they speak to each other in
Yiddish or Hebrew. There is an unwritten rule among their peers
never to speak to children in Yiddish, only Hebrew. But since
Yiddish is mixed with a great many Hebrew words, it is hardly
effective for telling secrets. So fortunately for them they have
another language in common, which is totally foreign to the
Middle East, namely, Polish. The only problem is, some familiar
words or names do pop up, and some emotional overtones are
hard to miss, and so the gist of what they talk about is not hard to
figure out, not even for an eight-year-old.

They are talking about the situation in the neighborhood.
We live on the edge of the main Arab neighborhood of Haifa,
known as the Lower Town, which stretches from the lower slopes
of Mount Carmel, where we live, down to the bay, and from
Wadi Nisnas in the west to Wadi Rushmiya in the east. Many
Jewish families living in our area have already left. Some have
been put up temporarily in school buildings in Hadar HaCarmel.
It was no longer safe for us to stay where we are.

As for me, I am too engrossed in that adventure book I am
reading about some treasure hunters in Africa. I am practically
swallowing every page. The events around me are too
troublesome for a child to dwell on. The idea of being afraid
doesn't not seem to faze me. In my imagination I am now in
Africa, far away from Jews and Arabs who are unable to get
along with one another. This Jewish-Arab conflict is too
tiresome. There are far more exciting things out there in those

exotic, far away lands, in places like the jungles of Africa, where there are lions and tigers and buried chests full of jewels and gold. We may be leaving the neighborhood? Well, perhaps next week, not today. Today I've got a good book to finish, which means that the world around me may fall apart, it will not stop me from finishing it.

23.

So here I am, right in the middle of the hostilities between the Jews of Haifa's midtown, known as Hadar, and the Arabs of the Lower Town, living in the middle of what is quickly becoming the battleground between the two camps, going about my daily life as if everything is perfectly peaceful and normal.

It is December, the beginning of winter. We children are playing in the empty lot between my house the adjacent houses on Luntz. All summer we have been playing marbles, shooting those colorful little glass balls in the dirt, in and out of the *jorah,* the little round hole we dug in the ground, trying to hit our opponents' marbles. Now that the rain started the ground became softer, and we were starting to play Nail. We would draw lines on the ground, hold a long construction nail by its head, and throw it in a fast, semicircular motion against the ground, so that the point of the nail would hit the line and remain stuck to the ground. I am not too good at either game. My head always seems to be lost in my books to pay too much attention to such trivial games. I am still somewhere in Africa or twenty-thousand leagues under the sea, with Captain Nemo. So I do my best to stay in the game, but I hardly ever win.

As we are playing, we start hearing the daily round of shooting. This time, however, it is more intense than usual. We can actually see those little balls of fire called tracer bullets flying up and down Sokolov Street, only fifty yards away. The spectacle is more interesting than our game, so we stop playing and we watch. One of us, who has an older brother, age fifteen, who serves as a courier for the Haganah, tries to explain to us what is going on. The Arabs have seized positions on the roof of the market building down the road, the market where my father delivers the fish crates. The Haganah has decided to dislodge those snipers from the market, and, in effect, to push the Arab positions further down the hill, away from the Jewish area. So they mounted a powerful machine gun, probably a Beza, on a building up Sokolov Street and started a barrage against the positions on top the market building.

When the shooting stops we each go home to stay closer to our parents. My mother is already in the street, looking for me. She seems relieved to see me unharmed, takes me by the hand and walks me home. I am told not to go out on the balcony overlooking Sokolov Street. It is too dangerous. I wait until my mother becomes busy in the kitchen to sneak out on the balcony. I edge along the wall and look out on the street. The street is deserted, when suddenly I see a young man running down the street waving his arms listlessly. There is blood streaming down from his face all over his shirt. For the first time I become scared. My knees begin to shake, and I quickly retreat back into the apartment. There is a war going on.

24.

The next day my father came home in the middle of the day and told my mother his truck had been taken away.

"By whom?"

"The Irgun."

"You let them take it from you?"

"They were armed. But they were very nice about it. They told me they needed it for a special operation for two days. They promised me they would return it on Friday, unharmed."

The next day we read in the morning paper the Irgun had pulled off one of its terrorist operations in Haifa. Irgun members had driven a truck up the mountain, carrying a barrel full of explosives. They unloaded the barrel and rolled it down the hill in the direction of the Arab neighborhood of Wadi Nisnas. The barrel exploded, shaking the entire neighborhood, and shattering windowpanes. It produced far more noise and smoke than damage. At the same time, Irgun members dropped leaflets in the neighborhood, written in Arabic, informing the Arabs the Jews had an atomic bomb. According to the report, quite a number of Arab families left town that day and moved away to a safer place, presumably Acre.

The next day my father's truck was returned, unharmed.

That Friday night my parents reached a major decision. They were going to buy an apartment in a new residential building which was being completed on the corner of Hillel and Balfour Streets, in a much safer part of town, farther up the mountain. At that point my father broke the big news to my mother: he had enlisted in the newly formed army, the Tzvah Haganah, or Defense Force.

My mother did not take too well to the news.

"You are thirty-nine, no longer a youngster. And you have

two children. You are not fit for active military duty. And besides, none of your friends at Tnuvah are joining. Neither Fritz, nor Moishe Futterman, nor Naftali Weisbrod, not even Yoskeh, the tough guy."

My father wouldn't budge.

"They need me," he insisted. "And they need the truck very badly. They have very little transport, which is a very big problem, once things get started in earnest. Wherever this truck goes I go."

"So who is going to support us?"

"I have figured it out. In the new building where we are getting the apartment there is store space for lease. We will open a small grocery store. You can never go wrong on a grocery store. It will keep us going until I am back on the job with the truck. Besides, as a veteran I'll get all sorts of benefits."

And so, on that Friday night in December, three momentous decisions were made in our household -- the new apartment, the new business, and, most important, my father became a soldier.

25.

My mother was right. By the standards of those days, my father was no longer a young man. Indeed, he was the only one among his friends at the food distributing cooperative, Tenuvah, who actually enlisted in the newly formed army. It was one more anomaly about him in what seemed to be an endless series of anomalies stretching back to my earliest memories. I've never known a person who did more things out of character than my own father. If I were to use him as a fictional character, no one would find him plausible. This may be the reason why I decided to write this personal memoir, rather than turn it into a work of fiction. My father was not a fighter. Unlike many of his friends, who thought nothing of getting into a fist fight now and then, a most common sight during my childhood years, my father was always the one who broke up fights. Once, when I was about four years old, I was sitting inside the truck next to the window looking outside at some young men fighting and throwing rocks at one another. One stray rock hit me in the temple (I still have the scar to prove it), and I started bleeding profusely. My father rushed at those young men and tried to punch the one who appeared to be their leader. The blow missed and the entire group, realizing what they had done, turned around and ran away. My father made a lame attempt to pursue them, but he soon stopped and came back, which was the smart thing to do, since I had to be taken to the nearest first aid station for some stitches (in those days they used metal clamps, the marks of which can still be seen under my left eye).

I wouldn't attempt to explain why my father, who was certainly no soldier material, and who had to feed three mouths besides his own, did such a thing. Was it conviction, patriotism, foolishness? Was it the fact that he was the only one among his peers who was self-employed and therefore had more freedom than the others to do what he wanted? Was it the fact that he did not want -- silly as it may sound -- to part with his truck, which he knew was going to be requisitioned? Did he need a respite from my mother's constant bickering? I never asked him this question, and even if I did, would he have given me an honest answer? Did he really know the answer himself? I sincerely doubt it. But this much I know: In the confusion of that time this was one more example among many of unusual behavior. It was a time, to borrow a line from an American folk song, that tried the souls of men (and women), and each person in the Yishuv made his or her own decision, and it was out of the sum total of those decisions that the state of Israel was born.

And here I must add one more observation, which was true of that time and which is probably true of all great moments in history, of all the wars and the revolutions and all those momentous events that shape the history of the world. Notwithstanding the fact that among the half a million of us the spirit of volunteerism and self-sacrifice was perhaps at its highest in all of Jewish history, not everyone was willing to do what was expected of him or her. In the book *O Jerusalem*, which relates with amazing objectivity and skill the events of this very same period in the Jerusalem sector, the authors tell us that when Ben-Gurion issued a call to the Jews of Tel Aviv to loan some jeeps or other four-wheel-drive vehicles to help break the siege on the holy city, all the jeeps in Tel Aviv suddenly were nowhere to be found. Hard as it is to believe, this was not at all uncommon. Self-interest, selfishness and greed were in abundant supply even during the most critical moments. In the final analysis, a few unusual individuals made all the difference in nearly every campaign and every critical moment during that period. I will single out some of those individuals later on, some of whom I've even known personally, and attempt to show how in each instance they tipped the scale, changed the fortunes of battle, and determined the outcome of the war.

Back to my father. He was now officially a soldier of the new army, which was now being pieced together from all the different groups that had been operating mostly separately, sometimes even at cross-purposes. Those included the Haganah, the Palmach, the Irgun, the Lehi, the Sea Units of Haifa, the fledgling air force, new units formed of Jewish volunteers from Europe and America, known as Mahal, and units formed from Holocaust survivors and Jewish immigrants from Arab countries, who were now arriving in our shores in growing numbers. This ragtag collection of characters will become in a few years one of the most formidable armies in the world, and will not only win wars but also serve as a human laboratory wherein the new nation will be forged out of immigrants from over one hundred countries, cultures, and tongues.

Even as I am saying all this, I fail to believe that out of characters like my father, and all the others I knew in those days, and my father's truck, and the ridiculous home-made weapons we had -- the Sten submachine guns (the exact antithesis of the Uzi) and the old rifles that kept jamming and the Davidka mortars that made more noise than damage and sometimes even managed to hit the mark -- that out of such a laughable disposition, in only a matter of a few years emerged one of the best organized, best equipped, most effective armies the world has ever known.

85

26.

Compared to our apartment on Luntz, the new apartment we were now moving into on the corner of Hillel and Balfour Streets was a palace. First, it had a standup shower stall, a novelty in those days. It meant you could take a quick shower standing up, and be done with it, rather than having to heat water, fill a tub, and go through the tedious ritual of splashing and scrubbing. Secondly, at long last our old icebox was going to be replaced by an American-made refrigerator. An electric refrigerator was everyone's dream in those days. It meant you did not have to lug heavy ice blocks from the ice vendor on the street up several flights of steps. It also meant you did not have to worry about the ice melting and the food spoiling. And for us, the children, the freezer was by far the best part. It meant we could produce our own fruit flavored frozen ice bars, which were a lifesaver during the long parched summers. And we could make all the ice cubes we wanted, without mother yelling at us we were wasting our parents' hard earned money. And to top it all off, we had the top floor apartment, along with which came the wide open roof, a sort of a private playground for me and my kid sister, clearly a city child's dream.

On the downside, the house did not have an elevator, and since we were on the fourth floor, we had to climb every day almost one-hundred and two steps (I once counted them).

I remember vividly the day we moved away from the frontline on Luntz and Sokolov to the safer rear on Hillel and Balfour. It was during Hanukkah, which was always my favorite holiday. My father was now wearing the makeshift uniform of the new army. He wore a French Foreign Legion round hat with a visor and a flap in the back which folded or could be let down to protect one's nape from the tropical sun. The hat was too small on him, and he wore it on a slant, which made him look like a dandy of sorts. He had a British military jacket, known as a battle-dress, with shoulder straps and several pockets, baggy khaki pants, and army-issue black hiking shoes, a size or two larger than his size 12. My mother was in a great state of agitation, what with her husband going off to war, the prospect of moving to a new neighborhood, running a grocery store, and taking care of two children. My four-year-old sister seemed oblivious to the entire scene, and as for me, I was rather excited to start a new life, although I was somewhat sorry to leave the frontline with all its excitement.

My father's truck was parked outside our apartment house entrance. We were saying goodbye to neighbors, and I told my neighborhood friends who gathered in the street I'll be back to play with them, but of course we all knew that was not the case. (One kid named Lifschitz I will meet again twenty-two years later, on the island of Curaçao, where the Israeli luxury cruise ship, the Shalom, happened to dock. He worked on the ship as a radio-communications engineer, while I was attending a convention in Curaçao of the Jewish communities of the Caribbean Islands and Central America. Talk about strange encounters! He still remembered the day we moved, after all those years!) My father had brought over a team of porters from the market to help load our belongings on the truck. One of the porters, I recall, was mute, and kept gesturing to the others. My mother felt sorry for him, and gave him a nice tip. Afterwards, I heard him talk to his friends in the street, telling them how he had fooled my mother.

I had to give him credit -- very few people ever managed to fool my mother.

Finally, in early afternoon, the truck was loaded down with

all our furniture and the rest of our household items. My mother and sister squeezed into the cab while I climbed up into the back of the truck with the porters. The truck made its way slowly up the street, and by the time we reached the steep climb of Balfour Street, my father had to go into low gear. By late afternoon we were all moved in. While my parents were trying to decide where to put each piece of furniture, I curled in my bed and started to read a book called *The Wonderful Adventures of Nils Holgerssons and the Wild Geese,* by a Swedish author named Selma Lagerlof. I read it in Hebrew, of course, not in Swedish, and I was completely absorbed in it. That Swedish boy, Nils, had some amazing experiences flying on the back of a goose, and that afternoon it was I who was seeing Sweden from that fascinating vantage point.

27.

It was the week of Hanukkah, my favorite holiday. What was it about Hanukkah I liked so much? I think in Haifa back in those days people had a special feeling for Hanukkah. Somehow everyone was deeply aware of the similarity between the events of Hanukkah during the time of Judah Maccabee, twenty-two centuries ago, and the events of our own time. We were the few against the many, exactly as the Maccabees and their followers were, and if they could win such incredible victories, so could we. In grade school we used to sing,

> *Our flag is raised high,*
> *Maccabees are we,*
> *We have fought the Greeks,*
> *And won our victory.*

Yes, we were all Maccabees, every one of us. This is what we were taught, and this is what we believed. This was our faith, and, as a child, I had no difficulty understanding it.

As soon as all the furniture was put in place we lit the Hanukkah lights. It was the only time during the entire year my mother actually participated in singing traditional blessings:

> *Blessed are You, O Lord, our God,*
> *Who has sanctified us through Your commandments,*
> *And commanded us to kindle a Hanukkah light.*

She had a good singing voice, my mother did, and I was sorry she did not sing hymns and blessings more often.

The next day I started making new friends in the new neighborhood. It was not difficult to make new friends during

89

Hanukkah, since everyone looked for partners to play dreidl with. All I had to do was go outside, crouch on the street corner and spin a dreidl. Soon a group of children my age gathered around and we started a game. We each put a few coins in the pot and each took a turn spinning the top. This one boy kept saying, I am no good, I have no luck, I'll never win. He had an exceedingly pained expression on his face, and I started feeling sorry for him. As he kept complaining, however, he kept winning, and wiped us all out. But I didn't care. I was making friends, and it was worth investing a few pennies in.

28

Shortly after we moved to our new home I started having difficulties urinating. It had nothing to do with the new apartment, which had a brand new toilet, but with my own personal plumbing, so to speak. My father took me to Kupat Holim, the health care organization nearly everyone in Haifa belonged to. After some tests it was determined I had a growth, or a tumor, in my urinary tract, which had to be removed. I was referred to the leading surgeon of Haifa, Dr. Peiser.

Dr. Peiser belonged to that group of German Jews we had in Haifa at the time, which was the closest thing our town had to an aristocracy. In this instance, Hitler's loss was our gain. After the monster came to power in 1933, some of the most prominent citizens of Germany left the country, and a rather distinguished group settled in Haifa. It included many professional people, doctors and scholars and experts in many fields. Some of them would become my teachers in high school. Some of those teachers had international reputations. They could teach in almost any university around the world, but instead they were stuck during those years with troublemakers like my friends and me. In any event, Dr. Peiser was a world-class surgeon, and my parents felt quite reassured entrusting the family jewels to him. My father was wearing his makeshift uniform when he took me to see the great physician. I recall how he stood in awe and trembling before the famed doctor when the nurse ushered us into his office. "Zeet down, Zeet down," Dr. Peiser bellowed, "no need to shtand."

We both sat down.

"Nu, vhat are you vaiting for?" Peiser roared, "take off your pants."

I did as ordered. The doctor put on his rubber glove and

began to examine my crotch.

"Mmm, mmm," he kept mumbling to himself, I see, I see."

My father looked at him pleadingly.

"Tumor," the doctor finally pronounced the dreaded word.

"Tumor," my father echoed. "Yes, Herr Doktor."

"Vee vill schedule him for Rothschild for next veek," he told my father.

"Thank you, doctor."

"Don't mention."

My father gathered up his courage to ask the much feared question:

"How much do I owe you for the visit, doctor?"

For someone like Dr. Peiser the sky would have been the limit, except that my father's limit was much lower than that, especially now, as he had stopped working.

Dr. Peiser's face turned red.

"Get out of here!" he shouted, pushing my father out of the office. "You expect me to charge a soldier at a time like this? You are villing to die for me, and I should charge *you*?"

My father took my hand, muttered a faint "shalom" and quickly cleared the premises.

The following week we all climbed into my father's truck and took the ride up Mount Carmel to Rothschild Hospital.

Of all my childhood memories, the week I spent at the hospital is among the most vivid. When we first arrived at the reception area, I had a glimpse of the long corridor that practically ran the length of that narrow, long building. Along the walls on either side there were wounded men lying on stretchers, with each one's feet practically touching the next one's head. Some lay still, others moaned, and one or two would let out a scream every once in a while. I later found out they had been brought here not only from different parts of the city, but also from nearby towns and villages which did not have full hospital services. These were the wounded of the war of independence which would start officially on May 14, 1948, when the State of Israel was proclaimed, but since the Arabs were too impatient to wait until then, it actually started on November 30, 1947, the day after the UN took its famous vote. Now the war was almost a month old. The worst of it, we were told, was happening in the Jerusalem area. But Haifa was certainly no safe haven either, as I was discovering for myself.

Dr. Peiser had his hands full. He was going non-stop day and night. Into this incredibly busy schedule he had to fit me, an eight-year-old who had trouble urinating. In retrospect, it sounds somewhat amusing. But when I sat in that waiting room at Rothschild with my parents, the last thing I felt like doing was laugh. The idea of having my insides cut with a scalpel was hardly amusing. I did not let my parents in on my feelings, knowing that they were not exactly thrilled about the whole thing. Besides, who was I to complain with all those men lying there bleeding from their wounds?

A nurse took me into a room with two beds. I was given the bed near the door, while the other bed, under the window, was vacant. I was told to take off my clothes, and was given a small white gown with straps that tied in the back. I was told I was scheduled for surgery later that afternoon.

Even now as I recall that day nearly half a century ago, I can still taste that paralyzing fear that came upon me. I lay in bed hardly able to move, as if I had turned into stone. When the two operating room assistants came in in their green tunics and white masks hanging down their chests, I closed my eyes and let them lift me and place me on the cart. They wheeled me down the hall

93

past all those wounded soldiers and into the operating room. When I opened my eyes I had to blink. I was staring at a huge round lamp with powerful light bulbs all around it. all turned on me. And then I heard Dr. Peiser shouting orders at his staff, his face masked, and his hands raised, waiting for instruments to be placed in them. And then another physician came over and put a rubber nozzle over my face and told me to count to ten. I started counting. With each count it became harder to breathe, and I was counting and whimpering and choking all at the same time. And then I began to spin, along with my bed and the entire room, spinning in the bright glaring light that went round and round, spinning like an airplane propeller at full speed, while half of the world became bright and the other half dark, and I was in the dark part trying to get away from the horror and pain of it all, over to the bright side where everything would be well again, not being able to do it...

When I woke up I was back in bed in my room. My hands and feet were strapped to the bed. I felt a dull pain in my groin. I sensed a rubber tube running from my groin to a bottle hanging from the side of the bed.

Several years later it was determined that two unfortunate things happened that day. First, there was not enough ether to go around, and so I was not given enough anesthetic to put me fully to sleep, hence that bad nightmare I was going through. Secondly, Dr. Peiser did not have enough time to operate on me, since there were several wounded men in critical condition awaiting their turn, and so he did not fully remove the tumor, which grew again, and had to be taken out again when I was fifteen. This time, I am pleased to report, all went well.

About an hour after I came to, one of the wounded men was brought into my room from surgery, and placed in the bed under the window. His leg was bandaged and stretched across the bed. He opened his eyes and gave me a sidelong glance.

"What's your name?"

"Morry."

"Amnon."

"Nice to meet you."

He asked me about my operation, and then proceeded to tell me he had been sent by the Haganah on guard duty near Wadi Salib, to keep an eye on the local Arabs and make sure no one tried to sneak up to the Jewish neighborhoods to place a bomb or shoot someone. While on duty an Arab sniper hiding on top of one of the buildings down that road of stairs shot him in the leg. He managed to get away and was picked up by a cab driver who brought him straight to the hospital.

Amnon was a very polite and soft spoken young man who was studying at the Technion, the polytechnical school which is one of Haifa's claims to fame. A few years later he would become an engineer and go to Sweden for an advanced degree.

I have been hospitalized several times over the years, in Israel, South America, and the United States. But no hospital experience ever compared to that stay at Rothschild Hospital in December 1947. Clearly, conditions at the hospital were chaotic, supplies ran short, and the staff was barely able to cope with the situation. Even a surgeon as prominent as Dr. Peiser could only do so much and no more. And this, mind you, was only the beginning of the conflict. It would get much worse later on, when the war was on full blast. But all of this is seen from hindsight. When I emerged out of that operating room I truly felt like a survivor, like someone who has come back to life. I had my notebook with me, and I started writing poems again, lying in that hospital bed, with little drawings on the bottom of each page.

I wrote mostly about nature, about all the beautiful things in this world that made life worth living. About Mount Carmel and Haifa bay and the deep blue sea, this lovely place I was fortunate enough to live in, so lovely people were willing to fight for, and die for, if necessary.

29.

During my stay in the hospital my parents managed to put together the grocery store on the corner of Hillel and Balfour. This was to be our safety net while my father served in the army. At first I was quite delighted by the whole thing, particularly by the candy section. But my mother issued a stern warning not to touch anything without her permission, knowing how difficult times were and how we all had to contribute to the war effort. She told me that while father was away I had to be her little helper, since a grocery store meant a thousand little details that had to be attended to. This part of it did not seem too appealing, but I knew she was right, and I promised to do all I could to help.

Soon we all learned the store was not going to be an easy proposition by any stretch of the imagination. Across the street on the next block was the Rubin Grocery. Mr. Rubin had been there for several years and had developed an expertise in obtaining a variety of products which were quite hard to get in those days, imported canned food, tropical fruits and vegetables, and other delicacies. He practically held a monopoly over food shopping in the neighborhood, and even had customers who came from some distance. To build up a clientele, my parents at first had to spend all day in the store wooing those few potential customers who happened to stop by. They treated each person with extreme courtesy (which was -- and largely still is -- almost unheard of in your typical Israeli store), hoping to befriend people and earn their trust. But those potential clients were not interested in courtesy or friendship, but rather in the kind and variety of products, and, of course, the price. We soon learned Rubin had started a price war, and was underselling us on almost every product. My parents, it appeared, could not compete on his terms, and making a living off of that store became a very tough proposition.

As time went on, food in Haifa became more and more scarce, and at one point became rationed. An austerity regime was proclaimed by the unpopular economic czar, Dr. Dov Joseph, and people were issued ration cards to limit food purchasing and consumption. The only ones who were profiting now from the food business were the black marketeers, who sold out of the back of cars, or in dark alleys, or on the go in public parks. Among those were many Holocaust survivors, who did not have a job, had not yet learned how to speak Hebrew, and, in some instances, might have acquired this illegal experience during and right after the war in Europe. The legitimate food merchants were under strict government control, and our store was subjected to frequent visits by the food inspectors, who carefully checked every drawer and shelf, most of which were empty, as if there were something to find. It reminded me of an old Jewish joke about Hershele of Ostropol, the proverbial shlemazel back in the old country, who was once awakened by his wife in the middle of the night and was told there were thieves in the house. Don't get upset, Hershele told his wife. I'll go down and help them search. Perhaps together we may find something of value.

For better or for worse, the grocery became the new focus of our lives, replacing my father's truck which had become part of the first Hebrew army in two thousand years. It would remain our focus for another year, until the war ended and my father returned to his family, bringing back his truck and resuming his fish transport business.

As for me, I continued to do the things all eight year olds do, and I kept following the events that were unfolding every day in our town and in the rest of the country, now from a safer distance.

Every day there was some action and counter-action somewhere in Haifa, Arabs attacking Jews and Jews retaliating against Arabs. It all came to a head the last week of December, when Arab workers at the oil refineries in Haifa Bay attacked unarmed Jewish workers and killed about forty of them. The funeral that followed was one of the largest and most somber I had ever seen. The whole town was in mourning. And then came the retaliation by the Haganah against the Arab village of Balad Al Sheikh, from where the killers came. According to official reports, it was a military action. But according to stories that circulated in the neighborhood, the Haganah chose a method of killing the Arabs with the same weapons they killed the refinery workers, namely, with knives and lengths of pipe, to make the message perfectly clear. A group of corpulent Jewish butchers was gathered by the Haganah and taken over to that village in the middle of the night. The slaughter that followed was designed to send a message to all Arab villages, that when it comes to slaughtering, Jews could do at least as good a job, if not better.

And so a new year -- 1948 -- began. It began ominously, grimly, fraught with the fear of the unknown. Arab leaders in the neighboring countries, we were told, had promised to throw all of us into the sea, come April, if and when the Jewish state was proclaimed. There was no going back now. From now on it was do or die.

30

As I look back it is hard to believe I went to school almost every day during that time, played in the streets with my friends, went to the movies, and gave my little sister a hard time. What else was I to do? I was too young to go to war, and my front was the homefront. So to make up for it I played war games. I took my air gun and went out on the roof of our building and guarded the building against air raids. Fortunately, the Arabs war planes never reached Haifa, any more than the Italian ones did during my infancy in World War Two, and I did not have to put my pellets or my darts to the test against Spitfires or Messerschmidts. To make up for the lack of action, I would go down to the yard and organize a battle between my friends and the kids from the next street, using rubberband slings and improvised catapults made of a board balanced on a rock, with a paperbag full of dirt and rocks on one end. We would drop a large rock on the other, higher end, and watch the bag go up in the air and land in front of our foes, creating a dust screen which enabled us to aim our slings and score some hits.

Some of those kids I played with went on to become some of the leading generals of the Israel Defense Forces. For whatever reason, Haifa is known to be a leader in producing high ranking military officers.

We did not see much of my father during that time. He was always off somewhere, on missions he could not talk about, no matter how hard my mother tried to pry out a hint or two. It was one of the most difficult times in my mother's life. Her husband was risking his life, and she had to work from dawn till dusk, trying to support the family. One evening after she closed the store we went upstairs to our apartment and she suddenly collapsed on her bed and started to cry in a way I had never heard her cry before. To me, she was always a pillar of strength, the most fearless woman I had ever known. I sat down next to her and started stroking her hair, telling her to stop crying.

"I can't stop crying," she finally managed to come out with it. "I just can't go on living like this."

I took her hand in mine and stroked it.

"What will happen to us?" she said between sobs.

I did not know what to say. Suddenly I was finding myself in the role of the man of the house. Little me had to comfort and reassure my formidable mother, who seemed to have lost her nerve.

"Well, Mother," I said, "I know how you feel. I feel the same way. We are like lost souls on a sinking ship. It's scary, isn't it?"

I could kick myself for having said that. It was not what my mother wanted to hear. She wanted to be comforted, not to hear about my own fears. Well, she must have caught me off guard, and I was clearly unnerved. Mother, if you can hear me, I am asking your forgiveness.

Well, you couldn't keep my mother down for too long. The next morning she was her old self again, full of spit and vinegar. She woke up my sister and me, packed us off to school, and resumed her duties at the store. Later that afternoon my father showed up and told us he had a two-day leave. He wanted to take the family for an outing, since we all needed a little change of scenery and some relaxation.

The next morning, on Saturday, we packed a picnic basket and took a ride into the wilds of Mount Carmel. Winter is a beautiful time of year on Mount Carmel, when nature is resplendent like no other time of the year. The slopes and fields

101

are dotted with red poppy flowers, pink cyclamens, white narcissus, bluebells, and many more wild flowers, and the scent of the pinetrees is everywhere. A family outing was always rare and precious in those days, and particularly now, in the midst of all our troubled existence, it was a gift from heaven.

After lunch my sister and I started scouting the area for some ball-shaped rocks known as Elijah's watermelons, a rare geological phenomenon which only seems to exist on Mount Carmel. My parents started a lively conversation, which I happened to overhear.

They were talking about the many problems they were having, and how difficult life had become. My father was saying that the first order of business was to win the war, otherwise we would all be done for. But after the war perhaps we ought to consider going to the United States, where we had many relatives, and start a business of selling fabrics, which my father's family had in Poland, and try to become more affluent. It was not the first time I heard my parents talk about going to America. My paternal great-grandfather, after whom I was named, went to America with two of his children early in the century, and gave rise to a large family. His wife stayed in Europe, raising the other children, including my father's father. After World War One, my father's father, who fought in the Austrian army, went to Ohio for four years, but his wife, my grandmother, did not want to leave her mother, and stayed in Europe, where she raised my father and his siblings. So this thing about going to America was deeply ingrained in my family history, and eventually I too would become affected by it.

Right now, however, no one was going anywhere. Right now a country was being born, and we, the midwives of this new country, had our work cut out for us.

31.

Yes, it was a long and difficult birth. Although Haifa, according to the UN partition plan, was included within the borders of the Jewish state, the population in the beginning of 1948 was about equally divided between Jews and Arabs, and it was hard to think of Haifa as strictly a Jewish town. If anything, Haifa was a cosmopolitan town. The city was surrounded by British military bases, and the harbor -- one of Great Britain's most strategic assets in this part of the world -- serviced ships and vessels from all over the world. When the new year was rung in, the British had started evacuating their forces from the Holy Land via Haifa harbor, and there was a constant movement of British troops through our town. At the same time, Arab irregular forces from the Galilee, from what is now the West Bank, and from as far away as Syria and Lebanon, had found their way to the Arab neighborhoods in and around the city, and were now preparing for the great battle that would see them become victorious over their Jewish foes. These irregulars became quite active in disrupting daily life in the town, throwing bombs, laying ambushes, and setting up snipers wherever they could along the major arteries, harassing traffic and passersby.

And here I must stop and tell you about a young man with very light, closely cropped blond hair, and only one ear. I can still see him standing in the aisle in the Amphiteatron movie theater in Haifa, on Hehalutz Street. He is standing there like a statue, not blinking an eye, not saying a word. He hardly ever speaks, and if he does, he only says a word or two. Years later, when I went to see the U.S. Senate in session, I saw Senator John Glenn standing next to one of the doors, observing the session, and his pose reminded me of that man back in Haifa in the Fifties.

I was suggesting before that a handful of people made all the difference in this war, which must be the case in any other war or major event in history. This young man was one of those few. In fact, he was one of the only twelve persons to receive the highest decoration of that war, the *Ot Hagevurah*, the Jewish version of the American Medal of Honor, which I believe was given to eight living persons and four dead, who showed unusual courage during the War of Independence. This man, along with another fighter who lost his life, in effect saved Haifa during the winter of 1947-1948, and opened the door to the Haganah victory in April, shortly before Passover.

The story goes something like this, as best as I could piece it together from both Jewish and Arab sources:

During the winter and early spring of 1948, both Jews and Arabs in Haifa were making feverish preparations for the imminent showdown. Both sides had a serious problem insofar as weapons and ammunition were concerned. During the British Mandate, carrying or possessing a firearm was punishable by death. The British authorities conducted regular searches for arms in the city and in the surrounding villages and kibbutzim, practically down to the last days of the Mandate. With its population about equally divided between Jews and Arabs, Haifa was a perfect example of a city where superior arms could tip the scale in favor of one side or the other. The Haganah and the Irgun had developed an elaborate system of clandestine production of arms and an intricate system of hiding those arms, taking them out of hiding without being noticed, using them in short skirmishes, raids and attacks, and then quickly returning them to the hiding places. The Arabs basically did the same thing. Both sides were manufacturing mines, timebombs, and large explosive devices in private garages, car repair shops, civilian factories, or in warehouses and barns, away from the suspecting eyes of the authorities.

As time grew near for the departure of the British and for the moment of truth regarding the viability of the new Jewish state, both sides began to look for ways to arms themselves in more serious ways than these guerrilla or partisan methods. The Jews had yet to start getting major arms shipments from abroad, which wouldn't happen for a few more months, and the Arabs were making arrangements in Beirut, Damascus, Amman and Cairo for quick arms purchases and gifts to bolster their positions in Palestine and start chipping away at the Jewish entity.

The commander of the Arab forces in Haifa, Mahmed al-Hamd al-Haniti, travelled to Damascus in the beginning of March, 1948, to prepare a major shipment of arms and ammunition for his forces in Haifa. Here is how Haj Muhammad Nimr al-Khatib, former deputy head of the Arab National Committee in Haifa, recalls the event:

> One of the most severe blows suffered by Arab Haifa -- which was an important reason for its falling into the hands of the Jews -- was the attack on the arms convoy near Kiriat Motzkin, and its destruction. In this attack the commander of Arab Haifa, Mahmed al-Hamd al-Haniti, was killed, as well as all the other members of the convoy (except for one, who was saved by a miracle).

> Here are some of the few details known about the destruction of the convoy:

> In early March al-Haniti arrived in Beirut, and after he spent some time with me he went to Damascus to obtain some arms and ammunition for the defense of Haifa. On March 17, 1948 he returned to Beirut to see me before his return to

105

Haifa with his weapons. Despite my pleading with him not to go with the convoy, the city commander insisted on doing it. He was joined by Sarur Barham, the commander of Eastern Haifa, who, like his superior, had also come to Beirut to obtain arms. The convoy consisted of two large trucks loaded with arms and ammunition, an escort car, the car of commander al-Haniti and his bodyguards, and the car of Barham and his wife. In Sidon a car semi-loaded with arms and ammunition destined for the command of the Jihad in Haifa joined the convoy.

The convoy reached Ras el-Nakura. This border post crawled with British and Jews, and there was concern that they might have told the Jews about the time of the convoy's departure. The convoy's commander had also made a serious mistake, which sealed its fate, by phoning his headquarters in Haifa from Ras el-Nakura and letting them know about his imminent arrival. The Jews, no doubt, intercepted the call and prepared to attack.

The convoy continued on its way to Acre. About 7 kilometers before reaching Acre they spotted a Jew slowly riding his motorcycle ahead of the convoy. After a few minutes he disappeared. When the convoy reached Acre, the dignitaries of the town and its warriors asked him to stay overnight and continue the next day, for fear the Jews might have laid an ambush for the arms convoy. Barham, the commander of Eastern Haifa, concurred with the suggestion, and advised sending the arms by sea from Acre to Haifa. Al-Haniti refused to listen and pressed on to Haifa. When the convoy reached the central square of Kiriat Motzkin, it noticed an armored vehicle standing across the road and blocking traffic. Before they were able to find out what was

106

going on, the first vehicle was fired upon, and its commander, a Jordanian officer who sitting next to a Bren machine gun, was covered with blood and collapsed. The people of the convoy immediately left their vehicles and took positions on the sides of the road. As the battle developed, one of the truck drivers was able to turn his vehicle and escape to Acre. He was followed by a car carrying the wife of Commander Barham, after the latter had left the car and joined the fight. The convoy people, who numbered less than 40 warriors, fell one by one, including the commander of the Haifa forces, al-Haniti.

When Bahram saw that there was no way of saving the convoy, he took out a hand grenade and tossed it on the truck to prevent the arms from falling into the hands of the Jews. The explosion caused the death of the rest of the convoy people, except for one, al-Haniti's driver, who was thrown in the air by the blast and landed at some distance on top of a train car on its way from Haifa to Acre.

The Jews also had considerable losses, at least several dozen, and many Jewish homes in the area were damaged.

The destruction of the convoy plunged Arab Haifa into deep mourning, and the National Committee published large mourning posters which called upon the population to take part in the military funeral arranged for the victims on March 18, 1948.

The Haj concludes his narration by saying:

With each passing day it became clear that Arab Haifa was on the brink of collapse. There was lawlessness and chaos everywhere. Many essential products were unavailable, including bread. Many fighters left their positions because of hunger. Worse yet, in those days when unity was so vital, the city was deeply divided and the disagreements cancelled out everyone's ideas.

Indeed, the end of Haifa was looming on the horizon.

Another Arab writer, Governor Sawa al-Hashami, wrote on March 18, 1948:

Today we received a telegram from Rashid al-Haj Ibrahim from Haifa. In this telegram he informs us that the Jews had attacked the convoy of Mulazam Mahmed al-Haniti, the commander of the garrison in Haifa, near Kirait Motzkin outside Haifa. The convoy was destroyed and Haniti and his men were killed. The Haifa commander was in Damascus a few days earlier to let those in charge know about the situation in Haifa. He was equipped with considerable amounts of arms and ammunition and left in a convoy with this precious cargo on its way to Haifa. The convoy's cargo included the following items:

40,000 bullets (French)
22,000 bullets (French, 8 mm)
26,000 bullets (English)
10,000 bullets (French, 10 mm)
19,000 bullets (German)
3,000 bullets (Tommygun)
10,000 bullets (Wably pistol)
600 Mils grenades
400 French hand grenades
550 French rifles with 5 grenade launchers
10 Wably pistols

2 mine detectors

2 tons explosives

For the sake of truth we may add that the late commander could have saved this precious cargo, which Haifa needed so badly, if he had transferred it by sea, knowing full well that the road between Acre and Haifa is strewn with Jewish communities, whose eyes are open, and there was no chance of bringing through a convoy without incurring a Jewish attack against it.

Furthermore, one must note with regret that those in charge of security in Palestine did not bother to keep the trip secret, which enabled the Jews to discover their movements in every town and village. In this regrettable instance as well the Jews knew about the movements of Haifa's commander, Haniti, and the equipment he had obtained. Was it any wonder, then, that Haifa fell within one day after its evacuation by the British, having been deprived of these most vital arms, which the military committee had such a hard time obtaining?

One must be very careful in reading Arab reports from those days. Facts are often mixed with fantasy, and exaggerations are very common. But the above two reports come remarkably close to the records of the Jewish side as to what took place in the central square of Kiriat Motzkin on March 17, 1948. What the Arab reports fail to bring out -- mainly because, it would appear, their authors were not privy to such information -- is the fact that the fateful convoy was, quite literally, stopped bodily by two young men, Emanuel Landau and Avraham Avigdorov (nicknamed Bumchik), whose incredible courage won them a year later the highest decoration of the war. According to the official report of the Haganah, Bumchik, age nineteen, emerged from his hiding place on the side of the road and confronted the first truck of the convoy within a few feet, firing his submachine gun at point-blank at the two machine gunners on top the truck, killing both of them. He managed to get himself seriously wounded in the course of this assault, and was evacuated by his comrades.

The other young man, Landau, ran under heavy fire towards the cab of the truck, reached the driver's seat, and started driving the truck away from the scene of the battle in an attempt to salvage the precious cargo. The truck exploded and Landau was killed on the spot.

The other young man, Bumchik, would spend months in a hospital where they would put him back together. His pre-battle picture shows him to be an extremely good looking young man, light blond with clean cut features. The doctors would do a good job saving his good looks, except for one ear which was blown away in that battle. In the early fifties everyone in Haifa would readily recognize the straight, blond, tacit young man, who, in recognition for saving Haifa was presented with a taxi-cab -- a coveted source of livelihood in those days. He was one of our living legends, a member of an exclusive club of only twelve young men in all of Israel -- eight living and four dead -- who did most unusual things at the most critical moments in that year-long conflict we Jews call the War of Independence, without which, more likely than not, there would be no State of Israel.

32.

The events I am about to narrate, which took place in Haifa in April, 1948, have been debated around the world for almost fifty years. The main reason for that is the fact that when the shooting stopped and the smoke cleared up, most of Haifa's 70,000 Arabs were gone, and the Arab refugee problem, which has plagued Palestinians and Israelis to this day, began.

I would like to piece together the events of that fateful month, from memory, from conversations with eyewitnesses, and from reading Israeli, British and Arab sources.

My own most vivid personal memory of that time is of those two days before Passover -- April 21 and 22 -- when my friends and I stopped playing war games and kept listening with awe to the constant explosions of bombs and grenades, and the firing of rifles, machine guns and mortars, which went on practically nonstop for two whole days and nights. We knew it was the real thing. We knew the fate of Haifa was hanging in the balance.

That memory is firmly linked in my mind with my childhood memories of Passover, so much so that for over forty years, whenever Passover comes around, I can still hear that endless cacophony of gunfire and explosions. I hear it most vividly during the Seder night when we read the Haggadah and come to the phrase, "Blood, and fire, and pillars of smoke."

And when we read, "In every generation one must consider himself as though he personally was redeemed from Egypt," I think of Passover 1948, when, at age nine, I saw my people rid themselves of foreign rule and become free people.

It appears that there were many players in Haifa in the drama of April 1948, Jews, Arabs and British. But what strikes me in particular is the extent to which most of what happened during that month was determined by the local leaders and the local populations, rather than by the Grand Mufti of Jerusalem, the leader of the Palestinian Arabs, or the British High Commissioner, who also resided in Jerusalem, or by our own leader, David Ben-Gurion, who had set up his headquarters in Tel Aviv at that time, where he was busy conducting the campaign to save Jewish Jerusalem, and preparing for the declaration of the establishment of the new state on May 14, when the British Mandate for Palestine officially came to an end.

This is important to point out, because for years we Jews have blamed the Mufti for talking Haifa's Arabs into leaving the town during the conflict, so that they might return later on after the victory of the combined Arab armies to reclaim their home as well as one abandoned Jewish home. The Arabs, for their part, have blamed Ben-Gurion and the Zionist leadership for deliberately forcing the Arab population out of its homes and turning it into refugees.

In reading Arab and British sources, it becomes apparent that in April 1948 there was little contact between the Moslem and Christian Arab leadership in Haifa and the Mufti in Jerusalem. Unfortunately, there is little original Arab documentation left in Haifa from that period, for, as I was told by the curator of the Museum of the City of Haifa, the Arabs in those days hardly kept any records. What is even more surprising, is the fact that Ben-Gurion, the leader of the Yishuv, had little contact with the Jewish leadership in Haifa during April, and did not find out about the Arab defeat until the next day.

I reread the three volumes of Ben-Gurion's diaries covering the birth of Israel and the war of liberation. From reading Israel's founder's diaries it becomes clear that during this period Ben-Gurion was very busy conducting the Jerusalem campaign from his headquarters in Tel Aviv, while the Haifa campaign was left in the hands of the local commanders of the Haganah, Moshe Carmel and Mordecai Macleff. Communications in those days between the north and the center of the country were very precarious. Jerusalem was virtually cut off from the rest of the country, and its fate became Ben-Gurion's main concern, while Haifa and the north were practically left to take care of themselves, first, because the situation there was not nearly as critical as it was in the Jerusalem and the Judean Hills sectors, not to mention the Negev and the south, which were awaiting the great Egyptian invasion, and, second, because there was only so much Ben-Gurion and the top leadership of the Yishuv could do with their scant weapons and meager supplies. In fact, the diaries make it very clear that Ben-Gurion was completely absorbed in finding supplies and weapons in Europe and in America, either through illegal means or through special negotiations with the Communist world, especially Czechoslovakia, which for the first and only time in the history of the Communist Bloc's relations with the Jewish state showed support for Israel (not for any altruistic reason, but because of Stalin's desire to see the British leave the Middle East, and his intention to bring Israel into the Soviet sphere of influence, which, of course, did not work out).

So, basically, the events I am about to narrate -- that 48-hour period on the week before Passover, 1948, those two fateful days during which Haifa became a liberated Israeli city, and half of its population, namely, the Arab half, became, for the most part, refugees, which started one of the most thorny problems of our time, those events took place strictly between us, the Jews of Haifa, and our Arab neighbors, with very little direction or influence from the national Jewish or Arab leadership. Without taking sides, I would like to examine the confusing events which

113

took place in my town during that time, and see what actually happened.

The confusion of those two days and the week that followed was not alleviated by the fact that two weeks later -- on May 14 -- a much greater event took place, namely, the proclamation of the state and the ensuing invasion of seven Arab armies. And so to this day no one is sure what exactly took place. Did the Jews force the Arabs out? Did the Arabs, prodded by their leader, the Grand Mufti of Jerusalem, choose to leave? Was it both, or was it neither?

The fact is that a day or two before the Haganah started that two-day decisive battle for Haifa, events in and around the city began to take on a life of their own, and neither the Jews, nor the Arabs, nor the British could do anything to change them.

In his book *The Birth of the Palestinian Refugee Problem 1947-1949,* which is certainly not tilted towards the Israeli side, Benny Morris writes that

> According to the British GOC North Sector, Major General Hugh C. Stockwell, the final battle was triggered by the town's Arab irregular units, who in mid-April 'went over to the offensive in many quarters... with the object tactically to push forward from two salients, Wadi Nisnas and Wadi Salib, to get astride Herzl Street, the main Jewish thoroughfare in Hadar Hacarmel.'

In other words, those irregular Arab forces, who were basically bands of armed militia, bandits, mercenaries, some of which -- as we found out later on -- were even headed by German Nazi officers who escaped from Europe after Hitler's defeat, found their way into the Arab community of Haifa, either at the

114

invitation of the local Arab leaders or on their own, and were now trying to shoot their way into the heart of the Jewish town -- Hadar Hacarmel -- where I was living at the time. It does not take a very vivid imagination to picture what would have happened had they succeeded in reaching Herzl Street.

During the time this took place, the British were in the process of evacuating the Holy Land. Haifa was their port of departure, and there was a continuous movement of British personnel and materiel through the Haifa harbor. The high command of the Haganah decided not to undertake any major military action in Haifa, so as not to upset the British or interfere with their evacuation. Haifa was left to the last, to be handled after the proclamation of the state.

And then a dramatic development took place. The British forces that were stationed between the Arab and the Jewish neighborhoods, keeping both sides from going all out at each other, pulled out, leaving a vacuum between the two hostile parties. What exactly was the British motive in doing so is hard to tell. One may argue that they were in the process of leaving anyway, and since they sensed that the two sides were about to go at each other in a big way, they decided to step aside and not incur any casualties of their own.

The future mayor of Haifa, Abba Khoushi (more about him later), who at the time was Ben-Gurion's representative in Haifa, went to see General Stockwell and told him that by giving up the buffer zone between the two populations, the British had allowed the danger of an Arab onslaught against the Jewish neighborhoods become real and present, and the Haganah wanted to know how the British felt about a Jewish preemptive strike. The general told Abba Khoushi the British were not at all in favor of it. Then again, one had to know how to interpret what the British really meant, as Abba Khoushi had learned over the years. Usually, their actions spoke louder than their words. While Stockwell was not going to give his blessing to any Jewish attack against the Arabs, he did in effect clear the field for a Haganah action.

The local Haganah leaders, Moshe Carmel and Mordecai Macleff, immediately pulled out Plan D, which was reserved for an unexpected emergency, as the new situation turned out to be. Previously, they had a different plan, code named Operation Scissors, which was designed as a tactical multi-pronged attack on the Arab irregular forces in and around Haifa, with the sole objective of weakening them and dissuading them from launching an attack on Jewish Haifa. Now a new operational plan was hastily drawn up, based on Operation Scissors, with the new name of Biur Hametz, the name of the Jewish tradition of getting rid of any remains of bread before Passover, so that the celebration of freedom can be observed by only eating matzah, or unleavened bread, for seven days.

This new plan had a new objective -- to take control of the entire area of Haifa. One could no longer wait for the British to leave. Action had to be swift and decisive.

The first major attack was planned against that three-story stone house down the road from the Wadi Rushmiya bridge, the bridge where my father almost lost his life a few months earlier. There was a very clear correlation between my father's risking his life on that bridge back in December, and the decision to launch the first major strike against that stone house controlling the bridge, known as the Najada House, at the outset of the decisive battle. Then as now, this bridge was vital for keeping communications open and transporting supplies between Haifa and the north of the country, namely the Galilee, the Valley of

116

Jezreel, and the northern coast. Both sides knew that whoever controlled that building held the key to the survival of the city.

The Najada House stands there to this day, an old Arab stone house with a bronze plaque commemorating the battle. To most people it signifies little, just another old house. But if you lived in Haifa in 1948, the words "Najada House" had a mythical ring to them, like the Bastille, or the Alamo, or Iwo Jima. As in most great campaigns, there is usually one landmark -- a house, a bridge, or a hilltop -- that comes to symbolize the entire campaign. All one has to do is utter that one word, and it immediately conjures up all the other events associated with it, the glory and the tragedy, the sound and the fury, and that cosmic silence that always seems to rest upon mythical places like the Najada House.

Quite possibly, the bullets that smashed into my father's truck six months earlier might have been fired from the Najada House, which has a good view of the bridge over Wadi Rushmiya.

In any case, when the battle for Haifa started, this house became the first objective of the Haganah. The three-story house was surrounded by a high stone wall and a heavy iron gate which was bolted and shut tight with a heavy iron lock. The place was guarded day and night, and there was no way of taking it without bloodshed.

The battle for the Najada House, at the eastern end of Haifa, was the opening round of the battle for Haifa. When it started, most of Haifa's Arabs were concentrated farther to the north-west, in the Lower City, near the harbor. A good number, including many of the Arab dignitaries and leaders, had already left the city, some were in the process of leaving, and the rest, to judge from the above-quoted and other Arab sources of the time, were praying for a miracle. The Arab irregular forces, scattered throughout the city, who only a few days earlier, according to the British commanding officer, were planning a push into the Jewish neighborhoods, were now engaged in a defensive battle against the Haganah units of the Carmeli Brigade, closing in on them from all sides.

The taking of the Najada House was planned as a quick assault aimed at dislodging the Arab defenders, and enabling the Haganah to control this strategic point. It turned out to be the most difficult task of the entire campaign, if one considers the fact that the small force that occupied the house remained under fire well into the next day.

One eyewitness and participant of that battle was my father's supervisor at Tenuvah at the time, Fritz Kalman. Both he and my father were members of the Haganah reserves. The Haganah at the time had two kinds of forces in Haifa -- actively trained units and reserve units. The trained units consisted of young men ages 18 to about 30, who were preparing to become combat soldiers in the new Israel Defense Forces, the official army of the new state. The reserves were men in their thirties and forties, who were given a variety of assignments, such as guard duty, security, logistics, and the like. When the campaign for the liberation of Haifa was hastily mounted on the eve of Passover, 1948, the Haganah made use of both kinds of forces. The combat units were brought in to conduct the actual campaign, while the reserve units were given the task of guarding the Jewish neighborhoods, businesses, factories and public utilities.

Fritz, as a reservist, found himself assigned to Beit Hataasiyah, or Industrial Building, a large cement building perched high on the slope overlooking Wadi Rushmiyah, practically at the point where Jewish Haifa ends and Arab Haifa begins. I spoke earlier about Wadi Rushmiyah, where my father's truck was hit several times by Arab sniper bullets. It was probably the most strategic point in all of Haifa (besides the harbor), since it was the only route connecting Haifa with the north of Israel. The British had just evacuated the Industrial Building, and the Haganah quickly occupied it and turned it into a small garrison, equipped with several mortars and machine guns.

Fritz was assigned to guard this building. He would later be wounded by shrapnel when the building took a direct hit, and I remember visiting him at a makeshift hospital on Mount Carmel. Now, nearly half a century later, he still winces when he recalls that battle.

It was terrible, he says. After the Haganah occupied the building it came under fire from different sources. Most surprisingly, it was fired on by the British, and took a direct hit from a British gun shell, which left a gaping hole near the top floor, while Arab snipers and irregular forces down in the valley and on the opposite hills kept firing at the windows from almost one hundred yard range, and kept going for hours. And if this was not enough, on the nearby ridges there were Iraqi units who had come to help their beleaguered brothers. They had several mortars which they aimed at the roof of the building, where Fritz and his comrades were ordered to take positions in order to provide fire cover for a platoon that was being dispatched around noon, on April 21, to take the Najada House. One of those mortar shells exploded on the roof and wounded Fritz in the leg. He was quickly treated by the medic and continued to operate the Bren machine gun, which was aimed at the houses firing on the approaching platoon.

From his vantage point on the roof, Fritz could see the

119

platoon being driven to the Najada House in two armored cars. From where he sat, high up on the Industrial Building, the two small makeshift armored cars looked like match boxes. He thought of the closing scene in *For Whom the Bell Tolls*, when Robert Jordan was laying the dynamite on that mountain bridge before the approaching Fascist forces. The two cars looked so puny, surrounded by enemy fire positions on all sides, located in those small Arab stone houses on the hillside on the right, up and down the street after the bridge, and all the way across the wadi as far as the railroad tracks. Could they really reach that house and take it?

The men of the platoon carried as many weapons and explosives as they could, but only little water and no food. One may speculate that their commander anticipated a short but fierce battle, which would necessitate all the firepower they could take along, but no food or water, except for the one canteen carried by the medic. It did not quite turn out that way.

Two squads, along with the platoon commander, Tzahi, went in one armored car, while the third, with the second-in-command, the radio operator and the medic, in the other. There had not been enough time to study the layout of the building and the surrounding houses, and so some details were left to chance.

The Najada House was surrounded by a nine foot tall cement wall, which had been erected by the Arab defenders a few weeks earlier after the LEHI had hurled a large explosive device into the house and shattered several walls. There was a breach in that wall, through which the platoon intended to enter the house. It was decided that the first armored car would drive in reverse and stop against that breach, and let the men go in through its back door.

As the armored cars moved towards the house, the Arab

120

defenders opened fire from all sides. The breach came under heavy fire, and was not accessible. It became necessary to seize the houses down the street, which were not surrounded by walls. Moving along the walls of those houses and across the yards, as the armored car moved next to the breach and shielded it from the enemy fire, the young warriors reached the breach and began to probe the entrance to the house. The first men to enter the house ran into two armed Arabs who engaged them in hand-to-hand combat. One squad commander was hit by grenade fragments as one of his men was shot. Both collapsed on the floor in pools of blood and lay still. The other men, all young with little or no combat experience, took cover along the walls as they were fired at from the second floor. The second squad commander, taking charge of the situation, began to toss grenades up the stairway, and soon they heard bodies fall down the steps with a thud. They cautiously proceeded up the stairs to the second floor, where one Arab sat on the windowsill and shot at them at point blank, nonchalantly, as he kept looking outside and shooting at the rest of the platoon members who were still in the yard. Stunned by his performance, the men stood there, when suddenly they heard him let out a cry and watched him fall out the window.

This ended the resistance inside the building. The attacking force went up to the third floor, stumbling over dead bodies, and began to take positions on the roof, as planned. Soon the men on the roof came under heavy fire from the Arab houses up the hill, and had to go back inside. They took positions at the windows on all three floors, with the main force staying on the first floor, to prevent enemy penetration.

The Arab fire intensified, emanating from only thirty yards across the street and from farther up the hills. Two men inside the house were wounded, and were placed on the bottom of the

121

staircase, which appeared to be the safest part of the house.

The Arabs appeared determined to recapture the house. Several of them approached the house from the front and the back and tossed grenades into the windows of the first floor, wounding several of the men inside. One grenade fell next to the wounded men in the staircase. Tzahi, the platoon commander, was able to catch it in time and threw it out the window. The first floor became unsafe, making it necessary to transfer the wounded to the third floor. The staircase became the command post, where the commander remained throughout the operation.

The Arab bullets kept slamming against the stone house from all sides. It was impossible to take aim through the windows and fire back. The only thing left to do was toss grenades with little or no aim, to prevent any approaching Arabs from reaching the entrance. One of the two surviving squad commanders rose to hurl a grenade, when he was shot in the head and was killed on the spot.

Meanwhile, Fritz and his comrades operated the mortars and machine guns on the roof of the Industrial Building, aiming at Salah A-Din Street, on the west side of the Najada House. But they could not reach the other, eastern side of the house, where the other prong of the Arab attack originated.

For the rest of the afternoon attempts were made to send reinforcement and evacuate the wounded and the dead, but to no avail. The commander of the besieged force had no trouble communicating with the sector commander on the roof of the Industrial House, since their respective positions made for good communication. He kept begging for help, describing the dire conditions of the men inside, particularly the wounded. With each barrage plaster from the ceilings and the walls showered on the dead, the wounded, and the living, entered their clothes, their eyes and their mouths. Fritz kept listening to the communiques and bit his lips. He knew some of those young men inside the Najada House. They came from some of the kibbutzim near Haifa, and, as a former member of Kibbutz Ein Gev, Fritz had watched many of them grow up. He was not a religious Jew, but he found himself murmuring a prayer.

Before nightfall the platoon was running out of ammunition. The commander ordered his men to save their fire and only use their weapons sporadically, to let the enemy know they were still holding out, and to keep up the spirits of those who were too weak to go on. The commander explained later on that he was beginning to panic, but he managed to keep a calm exterior so as not to let his men down. Meanwhile, another platoon was sent down the mountain from Tel Amal with the intent of occupying the house next to the Najada, but failed to do so because of heavy enemy fire. On the radio, the commander inside the Najada House asked to be evacuated. Nearly all of his men had now been injured in one way or another, and could no longer hold out.

Several attempts were made to send over armored cars for the rescue. They all came under very heavy fire. One was stopped by an illumination bullet, another took a hit in the gas tank, and a third was forced off the road.

By now all three squad commanders inside the house were dead. After dark the wounded began to moan and complain of the cold. Their comrades took off their sweaters and gave them to the wounded. It was a cold night, and the men without sweaters, who had not had any food or water since the day before, began to freeze.

Attempts to approach the house by armored cars continued till midnight. By now it became clear that the only way to rescue the men was to wait for the general offensive which was being mounted around Haifa to reach this sector. The commander was told that around one o'clock another platoon would approach the house as part of the general offensive, and join up with his. This lifted his men's spirits. In addition, the Arabs also seemed to be running out of ammunition, and their fire began to subside.

The relief force did not arrive at one o'clock. It reached the vicinity of the Najada House but was stopped by strong enemy fire, and had to fight for every inch of the way from where it reached the road. Its progress was monitored over the radio by the commander inside the Najada House, who attempted to brief the advancing men on where the fire was coming from. This continued almost till dawn. In the meantime, the general offensive had begun, and the Haganah was attacking the main Arab strongholds in the western part of the city, from Prophets Street down to the harbor. The word of the Jewish offensive began to spread throughout the Arab neighborhoods, and reached Wadi Rushmiyah as well. Many Arabs began to leave their homes under the cover of night and fled in the direction of the harbor. Some were caught in the crossfire between the relief platoon and the local Arab defenders.

But the fighting was not yet over.

In his book *The Northern Campaign,* Moshe Carmel, the commander of the Haifa campaign, writes:

Late at night I was in a position from where I could follow the desperate struggle of the besieged platoon, and from where we directed the operations of the units in this sector. We could see the house in the dark, less than fifty yards away, occasionally lit up by flashes of light. It was a very painful sight. Your fighters were nearby, with their wounded and dead, squeezed from all sides, and you could not rush to their rescue. The column attacking Halisa was receiving insistent orders to hurry up and come over to the house, even if it meant taking a risk, but while it kept advancing, its advance was maddeningly slow. We listened to the radio communications between the besieged and the attacking commanders, and we were touched to the core. The voice of the first seemed to shake, while the voice of the second was calming and reassuring. The besieged commander said,

'All my commanders are dead. I have more wounded. They are losing a great deal of blood and they are going to die. Please hurry up, go faster. Roger.'

The other commander replied:

'We're coming. We'll arrive. Hold out, hold out, hold out. Roger.'

'If you don't hurry up you will find all of us dead. We can't go on. There's no ammo. They are losing too much blood. There's no water. Please come. Roger.'

'We are very close, very close. Hold out. Roger.'

There were only a few yards between them, but it was an abyss of life and death.

A new day dawned. As the Arab masses continued to flee from the city and look for anything in the harbor that could take them across the bay to Acre and from there farther north, some of the Arab fighters around the Najada House refused to give up. They continued to fight during the morning hours, preventing the bleeding platoon from getting any relief or evacuating. Not till later that afternoon, as the fighting around Haifa began to subside, did the Arabs of Wadi Rushmiyah lay down their arms. Carmel writes:

I saw them when they arrived at their base. They came out of the armored car slowly, swaying from side to side as they walked, as if the ground under them was shaking. Their clothes torn, they were grey and tired, and their eyes seemed to wander, as if they were not sure of what was going on around them. Their commander, a tall well built young man with burning eyes, was somewhat bent and there were small wrinkles on his dark forehead. As he walked into the barracks he said quietly, casually to the base commander, pointing at the armored car,

"In the car there are two more dead persons from my unit. Please attend to them."

Map of the battle of Haifa

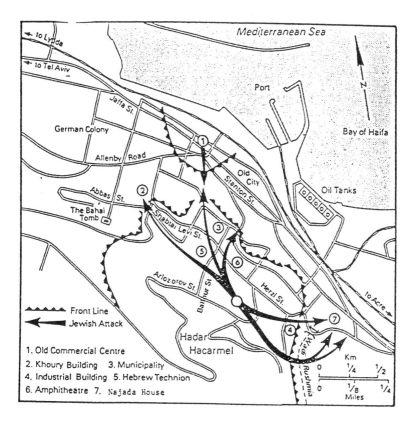

Front Line
Jewish Attack

1. Old Commercial Centre
2. Khoury Building   3. Municipality
4. Industrial Building   5. Hebrew Technion
6. Amphitheatre   7. Najada House

33

The Arabs fought valiantly in Haifa, and so did we. There was one big difference between them and us, which was characterized by the Classic Israeli expression, *Ein breirah*. In other words, we had no choice. We had no place to go. They could flee to Lebanon, or Syria, or any other number of places. We fought, so to speak, with our backs to the sea. They had vowed to throw us into the sea, and we knew, especially after Auschwitz, that it was no false promise.

I chose to describe in the previous chapter what was perhaps the most dramatic and heroic episode in the battle for Haifa, on both sides. The rest of the battle was less concentrated or dramatic. Essentially, the Haganah put a great deal of psychological pressure on the Arab population by broadcasting in Arabic over the Voice of the Haganah and circulating on the edges of the Arab neighborhoods in vans with loudspeakers, letting the Arabs know all approaches to the city had been seized and no reinforcements could reach Arab Haifa. It was best for the irregulars from Syria, Transjordan and Iraq to go home, and for the local Arabs to lay down their weapons.

Indeed, the Arabs lay down their weapons sooner than expected. The Haganah commander, Carmel, was stunned to hear from the British commander, Stockwell, on the morning of April 22, while the fighting at the Najada House was still going on, that the local Arab leaders wanted to know what the Jewish terms of surrender might be. Was it a ploy? Were there Arab forces from the neighboring countries secretly arriving in Haifa, perhaps by sea, possibly under British auspices, and while the Haganah relaxed its vigilance, those forces would suddenly attack?

But there was no time for speculation. The state of Israel

was about to be announced in Tel Aviv, largely on faith, and claiming Haifa would be an excellent justification for such an announcement. Brigade Commander Carmel proceeded to jot down the surrender terms. He had a feeling of "wasting precious time in the midst of all the fighting," but nevertheless, purely on faith, he sat down and wrote:

a. The Arab forces surrender to the Haganah and turn over all weapons, ammunition, explosives and other materiel, including armored vehicles.

b. All foreign fighters, including German, British, Yugoslav and other commanders who are in town will be turned over to the Haganah and taken prisoner.

c. The Haganah will take control of the city and all inhabitants will obey its orders and enjoy its protection.

d. All residents, Arabs and Jews, will have equal rights and duties.

e. A curfew will be imposed immediately on all Arab neighborhoods. Everyone will stay at home, and anyone who has a weapon will bring it to a designated collection point.

f. All foreigners will assemble in designated areas.

g. Anyone who offers armed resistance or is found to have a weapon in his possession after the deadline, may be shot.

And so, while fighting was still going on between Haifa's Arabs and Jews, representatives of the Haganah, the British forces, and the local Arab leadership, met at the beautiful stone and marble city hall of Haifa, where for thirty years Arabs, Jews and British ran the city in harmony on a rotation basis. This year the mayor happened to be a Jew named Shabtai Levi, a peace loving man who was quite popular among all the parties.

Stockwell presided over the meeting, and seemed pleased to meet, for the first time, a senior Haganah commander, namely, Mordecai Macleff, Carmel's Operations Officer, who would later become chief of staff of the Israel Defense Forces. Indeed, it was the first time a Haganah representative met at the negotiating table with Arab and British counterparts. Carmel himself was busy conducting the battle for Haifa, while Macleff took some time out from his operational duties.

The Arab representatives were Moslem and Christian Arabs, including Victor Khayat, who owned Khayat Beach south of Haifa, one of my and my friends' favorite beaches in those days. He also owned the bus line that went to that beach, and I understand that he owns a great deal of real estate in Haifa to this day. The Jewish representatives included Shabtai Levi, the mayor of Haifa, and a few other local leaders.

General Stockwell read the Haganah's terms of surrender to the assemblage. The Arab delegates asked for an hour and a half for consultation.

Everyone dispersed, and at the appointed time the meeting reconvened at city hall. The Arabs were not there, and since one could still hear isolated fire coming from the direction of the lower city, the Jewish delegates began to wonder whether the Arabs would show up at all.

Two hours later they did show up. They walked in in their suits and ties, and sat down quietly. Their spokesman got up and said they could not accept the terms of surrender, since they had no control over the fighting elements, and even if they did accept the terms, they could not impose them. They preferred to leave the city along with the rest of the Arab population, men, women, and children. (According to Carmel, they had just gotten in touch with the Grand Mufti, and were ordered to leave the city rather than surrender, since the invasion of the Arab armies was imminent, and they would soon be able to return. While I have no reason to doubt Carmel, whom I have always known to be a man of great honesty and integrity, it seems to me that regardless of what the Mufti had to say, the leaders of Haifa's Arab community spoke the truth. They were not in control of the situation. The mass exodus of the Arab population had been in progress, and the waves were turning into a flood, which they could no longer stop, nor, for that matter, could the Mufti. From everything I have heard and read, they all feared for their own lives, and did not feel empowered to sign any surrender documents).

The elderly mayor, Levi, got up, visibly shaken, and asked the Arabs to reconsider. Why would they want to leave the city where their families have lived for centuries, where their ancestors were buried, and where for so long they have lived in peace and harmony with their Jewish neighbors?

Stockwell, according to eyewitnesses, turned pale, and said to the Arabs:

"Don't make such a grave mistake. Reconsider it, for later you may regret it. You should accept the Jewish terms, which are perfectly fair. Don't destroy your lives unnecessarily. After all, you started this conflict, and the Jews won."

He turned to Macleff and asked:

"What have you to say?"

"It's up to them to decide," Macleff replied.

131

34.

One thing does emerge from the Jewish eyewitness accounts of the battle and its aftermath, and from my own personal recollections of the period. We the Jews of Haifa in the beginning of April, 1948, were not so presumptuous as to believe that we had the power or the will to dislodge the entire Arab population of Haifa, and turn Haifa into a Jewish city. Our first order of business at the time was to survive the Arab onslaught and to ensure that the Hebrew parts of Haifa -- Hadar Hacarmel, Mercaz Hacarmel, Ahuzah, Bat Galim, Neve Sha'anan, and so on, remained ours. We never doubted for a moment that Haifa was a city shared by two peoples -- Jews and Arabs. Since Haifa was included in the Jewish part of the UN Partition Plan, our objective was to prevail in an armed conflict with our Arab neighbors and validate our sovereignty over the city, with its Arab population continuing to live next to us as before.

One should bear in mind that Haifa was the main stronghold of Jewish socialism in Israel, and one of the key principles of Jewish socialism at that time was the Marxist idea of the so-called "brotherhood of nations," which meant that Jewish socialists were out to prove to the world that they could find a way for Jews and Arabs to live side by side in peace. One could almost go so far as to say that it was the interest of the Jewish leadership in Haifa to see the Arabs stay under Jewish rule and to show the world that Jews could dispense justice and equality to all people.

And then, of course, there were practical considerations. Arabs provided many of the services in and around Haifa. While we still lived on Luntz Street, prior to November, 1947, an Arab woman named Fatimah used to come to our house and help my mother with the house chores, which was quite common in those days. It was almost impossible for us in those days to think of

Haifa functioning without Arabs. We interacted with them on more levels than could be counted on both hands, and more than in any other part of Israel, with the exception of Jerusalem, we all accepted the premise that there were, in effect, two Haifas -- a Jewish one and an Arab one.

But history makes its own rules, and we humans are forced to live by those rules. Soon we were becoming used to the idea of a new Haifa, one where few Arabs were left, and many Arab homes stood empty. It was not a time of soul searching. The real war was around the corner, and its outcome was unknown. One thing we did know -- some of our fathers, brothers, friends, neighbors would not return from that war. The question was how many.

And there was one more thing to consider -- Holocaust survivors were arriving in Haifa by the boatload, as well as Jewish refugees from the neighboring Arab countries. They all needed homes. We did not have the means to provide them with homes. Here, all of a sudden, there were many vacant homes. I still remember as a child feeling the injustice of it all. But, as I said, it was not a time of soul searching. It was a time of war.

35.

The first Passover in liberated Haifa was not all that memorable. No one seemed to be in a celebrating mood. The war was about to begin in earnest, and the uncertainty was overwhelming. Our Arab neighbors had promised a major invasion by seven Arab armies -- Egypt, Syria, Transjordan, Lebanon, Iraq, Sudan, and Saudi Arabia. They had vowed to push us into the sea, and be done with us. We had no reason to doubt them. They were totally opposed to the UN resolution for the partition of Palestine into a Jewish and an Arab state. The battle for Haifa had been a local affair between us and the Arabs living next door to us. It was basically guerrilla warfare between two irregular forces, the Haganah and the Arab gangs, as we called them. It was only a prelude for what was yet in store for us. So as we sat to celebrate the Seder the week after the battle of Haifa, there was great apprehension among the grownups, which we children could sense.

I might add that my parents and their friends in those years did not pay much attention to the Seder in the first place. The fact that they celebrated the Seder altogether is something that needs explaining. It was the only time during the year they actually went into any trouble to prepare for a Jewish event that involved prayers, traditional singing, and a festive Jewish meal. Back home in Europe they sat through a long-winded traditional Seder during which their father invariably mumbled the prayers endlessly and put them to sleep. They were not going to do the same thing to their children. Instead, they would open the Haggadah, glance at a couple of pages, mumble a few hurried words, close it, and turn to the meal. The rest of the evening consisted of small talk and a little bit too much wine and the stealing of the Afikoman, and would quickly conclude the ritual part of the Seder. They did not use separate dishes for Passover, they did not care if the wine was Kosher for Pesach or not, they were not interested in any of the ritual minutia. We ate matzoh, of course, and we drank red wine, and we had the symbols of the Seder -- parsley, hard boiled egg, salt water, shankbone, horseradish and haroset -- on the table, but unlike our grandparents in the Diaspora or our coreligionists in the rest of the world, we did not dwell so much on the exodus but rather on the present moment -- our own exodus, our own struggle to create a Jewish state. In short, we did not sing, at the end of the Haggadah, "Next year in Jerusalem" (we never reached the end of the Haggadah, for that matter). Rather we thought of our fellow Jews in Jerusalem who had the task of rebuilding the city so that it may serve once again as the eternal capital of the Jewish people.

A couple of weeks later I saw the headline in the daily newspaper, the Ha'aretz, announcing the birth of the state. In the large photograph, the balding man with his white halo of hair stood under a huge picture of the Dr. Theodor Herzl, the visionary founder of political Zionism, and read the Proclamation of Independence to the assemblage of the leaders of the Yishuv. We also heard him over the radio. He spoke Hebrew with a heavy Russian accent, tinged with a little bit of an American accent. The Russian accent was no surprise, since he hailed from Russia. The American accent was a little harder to explain. He did spend some time in the United States in his younger days, but not enough to acquire an accent.

As a child I learned how to imitate Ben-Gurion reading the Proclamation of Independence. It was good for a few laughs, but it was also a privilege to be part of history, to repeat words that changed the lot of the Jewish people in this world forever.

135

But here again there was no special celebration. Unlike November 1947, when the UN vote became known, this time there was no dancing in the streets and no celebrating going on for days. Everything was ominous. American leaders had counselled Ben-Gurion to postpone the proclamation. It was too soon. The Jews did not have enough resources to ward off an Arab invasion on all fronts. The infant state could die in its cradle. Ben-Gurion stood fast. He knew we had to seize the moment, not lose the momentum we had built since November. He knew many lives would be lost. But he also knew it was the price of independence. No one was going to hand the Jews a state on a silver platter, except for their own sons and daughters who were willing to lay down their lives for their people.

And so the happiest moment in David Ben-Gurion's life was a grim moment. Like Lincoln in Carl Sandburg's biography, standing on the bank of the Potomac on the eve of the Civil War, peering southward into the dark night, facing the most fateful decision of his life, so too our leader knew he was making the greatest gamble of his life, putting the fate of the Jewish people in the balance, and for the first and only time in his life this non-religious Jew uttered the words, "The Rock of Israel," knowing that there comes a moment in everyone's life when only a higher power can be counted on to win.

As I wax poetic over this whole thing, I also remember that even as a child of nine (I turned nine in March of that year) I sensed all those things. Every one of us did, regardless of age. Everyone could feel history being made, and everyone knew a price had to be paid, a terrible price, and people were ready to pay the price.

And so the Arabs invaded. Their tanks rolled into the kibbutzim in the south, into Yad Mordecai (named after Mordecai

Anilevitch, the young leader of the Warsaw Ghetto uprising, who died in battle against the Nazis on Passover 1944), and into Negba, and Nitzanim. The Syrian tanks rolled into the kibbutzim in the north, Degania, and Mishmar Ha'emek. And the armor of the Jordanian Arab Legion rolled into Jerusalem. And I remember the young men of Haifa lining up at the recruitment centers, given their uniforms, some even given a rifle, and I can still see them piling into buses and trucks near the main entrance to the harbor on Kings Street, as they were going to the front. As the bus pulled out they all burst into song. They sang,

> *Believe me, honey, a day will come*
> *All will be well, I promise you,*
> *I'll be back to hug and kiss you,*
> *And make you forget all about it.*

Many of them would never come back. But they all sang, and when I saw them about to leave for the front they were all in high spirits. And if we live today it is because of them. They were "the boys," as we called them. I don't believe there were ever boys like them, or ever will be again. They gave their all, and, in the words of the poet, they were the "silver platter" on which Israel was offered to us.

36.

My father was now gone for weeks at a time, and my mother was a nervous wreck. Every day there was a list of casualties, and everyone was afraid to open the newspaper or answer the doorbell. One day my father came back in the middle of the day. My mother and I were in our grocery store, and there he was, wild eyed, a week old stubble on his cheeks and chin, standing there in his uniform, hardly able to talk. My mother must have been frightened by the sight. Typically, she would start harassing him for being so dumb and going to the war when he was supposed to be home with his wife and children. Needless to say, he would get very upset and told her she had no business carrying on like this.

I wasn't told much about what he had just been through. All I knew was that he took part in some major battle in the Galilee, in a place called Nebi Yusha. Over the next several years I would learn bits and pieces about what he had experienced. It actually took him several years to bring himself to talk about it. Basically what happened was that he drove a unit of young Palmach men to that British police fortress called Nebi Yusha, which controlled one of the main roads of the Galilee. James Michener describes this battle in his book about Israel, *The Source*. It was a difficult battle. The wall of the fortress had to be breached to get inside and take the place. Several men were killed, including the nephew of a good friend of my father's. "I told him to be very careful," my father would tell me years later. "He said to me, Zvi, don't be silly, the Arabs don't know how to fight. We'll go over there and take that place and everything will be okay." He was only right about the first part of his answer.

For the next several months, I and my friends, who had just lived through the local fighting between Jews and Arabs and the

138

showdown of April, became passive watchers of the official War of Independence that was unfolding in other parts of the country. Every day we would listen to the news, and every day we would read avidly every report in the papers. To this day, Israelis are compulsive newspaper readers and radio news listeners. I think this trait goes back to those days in 1948, when our lives were constantly hanging in the balance.

One Israeli poet, Shin Shalom, described that time as living on "high voltage." We all lived on high voltage, including the children. We were all mobilized, every single one of us. "The entire country is a front," was one of the expressions I remember from those days.

37.

One of the heroes of my childhood was Vladimir Jabotinsky. Who was Jabotinsky? A legend, a renegade, one of the greatest leaders we Jews have ever had, and also one of the most maligned and misunderstood. In a word, the perfect romantic hero.

Jabotinsky once wrote, "There is an old custom among the daughters of my people. When they are about to be married, they shave their head, and they don a wig. It is a most beautiful act of love performed by a woman. She sacrifices the crown of her beauty for her beloved. So have I shaved my head and dedicated my life to my people."

I have since learned that other people do the same or similar things. The best known, perhaps, are Catholic nuns, whose hair is shaved off before they are initiated into their order.

And, of course, the daughters of Israel who went to redeem the land of Israel gave up this custom as backward and barbaric. And many a modern Catholic frowns upon the medieval strictures of the Church. But when I think of the way we were in 1948, I am hard put to find a better metaphor than my grandmother's shaven head, which in a way made her into a Jewish nun. None of us shaved our head, or, for that matter, any other part of our body. But we did many other things which put us out of the ordinary run of life and made us into an ascetic order dedicated to a single goal.

One may wonder what in the world I am talking about. Well, I see us back in 1948, the way we dressed, walked, talked, acted. The women wore very little if any makeup. As a child I never saw a woman wearing a fur coat, and hardly ever any jewelry. Men wore khaki shirts and pants and simple leather sandals, or, if necessary, heavy work shoes. I recall a poem of that time by one of our great poets, Avraham Shlonsky:

Dress me, mother dear, in those resplendent clothes,
And at dawn show me the way to work.
My country is wrapped in light like a prayershawl,
Houses stand like phylactery boxes.

What resplendent garment and which mother was Shlonsky talking about? Not an actual garment and not his own mother whom he had left back in Russia. The mother here is the land, and the beautiful clothes are the sunshine, which is as white and as clear as a new prayershawl, and the landscape itself, which envelopes the poet-laborer like the most beautiful apparel.

The love affair between us and this land was so intense that we felt no need to make ourselves look attractive. The land itself was attractive enough, and we were part of the landscape. The land made us beautiful, and that was good enough. The land was the queen, and we were her servants. Our clothes were the colors of the land -- brown, blue, white. Unconsciously, we imitated the land, made ourselves look like her, the way a daughter imitates her mother.

I never sang for you, my land,
I didn't glorify your name
With mighty deeds
Or bravery in battle.
A little sapling my hands planted
On the silent Jordan bank,
A little path my feet made
Across the fields.
Indeed, how poor my offering,
I know, dear mother,

Indeed, how poor
Your daughter's gift.
Only a shout of joy
The day the light will shine,
Only hidden tears
For your misery.

Thus sang Rachel, one of the early pioneers in the land of Israel, who died young, and whose short poems became part of the soul of Israel. Like Rachel, we all felt unworthy of the land, and many of the poems of the time reflect these feelings of unworthiness. We also used to sing by way of apology to the land,

Our silos are filled with grain
Our wineries with wine,
Our homes with the sounds of the newly-born
And our cattle is fertile.
What more will you ask of us, our land,
What more is missing?

Our one goal, in the words of the *Hatikva*, which now became our national anthem, was "To become a free people in our land, the land of Zion and Jerusalem." For that goal we were now fighting, and we, the same Jews who only three years ago were butchered in Europe by the millions, were bodily stopping seven Arab armies.

Yes, bodily. I already told the story of twenty-year-old Avigdorov, who bodily stopped a weapons convoy on its way to Haifa, thus saving the city, and only saved his life by a miracle. I would like to mention a few more boys, out of many, who did similar things.

First, there were the few boys in kibbutz Yad Mordecai, named after the leader of the Warsaw Ghetto uprising, Mordecai Anilevitch, members of his organization, Hashomer Hatzair, who founded the kibbutz during World War Two in his memory. They sat in a trench outside their kibbutz, situated on the coastal road from Egypt to Tel Aviv, and watched an Egyptian armored force approach their trench. They only had a few rifles, limited supply of hand grenades, and a light machine gun. They were outnumbered, outgunned, facing armored vehicles. They stopped that force and made it retreat several times. They were bombed from the air. The entire kibbutz went up in flames. They refused to give up. They held off the Egyptian force for five days. By doing so they gave Tel Aviv a chance to prepare for the attack. The Egyptian invasion of Tel Aviv, aimed at throwing its inhabitants into the sea, failed because of a few boys in a trench on a landfold outside kibbutz Yad Mordecai. On the sixth day the kibbutz was overrun, but the Egyptian attack was no longer a breakthrough, and Tel Aviv was saved.

In the north, a column of Syrian tanks came rolling off the Golan Heights and entered the gates of kibbutz Degania, on the banks of the Sea of Galilee. A few boys engaged the tanks with light weapon fire, but were not able to stop them. Finally one of them rose with a Molotov cocktail in one hand and tossed it against the turret of the tank. The tank was set on fire, and stopped. All the tanks behind it panicked, turned around and escaped. Degania was saved, and so was the Galilee.

In Jerusalem there were countless stories of this nature. Some were recorded in the aforementioned book, *O Jerusalem*. Most of them are recorded in the history books. Every stone in Jerusalem is soaked in Jewish blood, going all the way back to

King David. Jews fought for Jerusalem throughout the ages, against many a foreign invader. Jerusalem was destroyed, burned, razed to the ground by the Babylonians and by the Romans. Jews and Arabs fought each other for Jerusalem since the beginning of the present century. And in the War of Independence both sides fought valiantly for it, the Arabs no less so than the Jews. I have seen Arabs pray at the Omar Mosque and at the Al Akhsa Mosque on the Temple Mount in Jerusalem. Their fervor was no less great than our fervor when we pray at the Wall. It was in Jerusalem that their prophet, Mohammed, went up to heaven, and so Jerusalem is nearly as holy to them as Mecca and Medina. But Jerusalem happens to be the eternal capital and spiritual center of the Jewish people since time immemorial. And although the Jews were badly outnumbered and outgunned in Jerusalem in 1948, they fought their greatest and most bitter battles in this part of the country. We lost the Old City, but we kept the new city. Thousands of boys from all over Israel, including hundreds of newly arrived Holocaust survivors, fought in the long Jerusalem campaign in 1948, and many died. But Jerusalem was saved, albeit a mutilated city with barbed wire running through her heart till 1967.

All this, of course, sounds very heroic and very romantic. After the fact, perhaps it is. But in 1948 it was very different. It was a grim time, grim and tragic.

38.

The war of independence, which started officially on May 15, 1948, continued into 1949. In March 1949 I became ten years old. I remember feeling awkward about turning ten. I was no longer a little boy, certainly not in the context of that place and time, when eight and nine year olds were serving as couriers for the underground and later for communities under siege. I remember thinking to myself, I was about to become a teenager, but I wasn't there yet, and I was no longer a little child. I was in some sort of no-man's land. I felt it was a cruel thing to do to a child to make him become ten years old. One should skip from, say, eight to thirteen. That would make much more sense than turning ten. But apparently no one had any control over such things. One had to become ten after being nine for one long year which never seemed to end, and wait patiently till one became eleven, twelve, and thirteen. But patience was not one of my greatest virtues. And so at ten I turned inwardly, into my own world of books and fantasy and writing poems and keeping a diary. I wrote things without any special reason or purpose, simply to be writing. Thus, for example, I recall writing a diary of the Korean War which I kept well into 1950, an activity which has puzzled me ever since. Why would a Jewish boy in Haifa in 1949 or 1950, in the middle of such momentous events taking place in his own country, keep a diary of a war thousands of miles away, which had nothing to do with him or with his fellow countrymen?   I recall reading the newspaper every day and following every detail of that war, and then writing my own report and comments on the progress of that conflict. But that was me in those days. I was completely absorbed in my books and in my newspaper reading and in my studies, a bookworm par excellence, a straight A student, winning all the honors my school

145

and my social and cultural environment had to offer to a ten year old.

Certainly my parents -- particularly my mother -- were quite proud of me. My mother would show my report cards to all her friends and to anyone who cared to see them. It was my way of contributing to the war effort -- making my parents proud and lifting their spirits, showing them that there was a purpose and a reason for all that struggle, all that sacrifice, for they were doing a good job creating the New Jew, the new person to be known as "Israeli," who would wipe out the shame of the long exile and enable Jews to become proud and free people who could hold their heads high and take their rightful place among the nations of the world.

And so, like Sir Francis Bacon, I made all knowledge my province, and I became the king of bookworms, a walking encyclopedia, a writer for all seasons, in short, an introverted and reclusive kid with an inflated self-esteem which was, unfortunately, supported by parents, teachers, and even schoolmates, who accepted me as the star student of the school, and were proud to be my schoolmates, since all their mothers, all those Jewish mothers, were always telling them, "Take an example from Morry Schreiber, try to be like him."

In January 1949 we knew we had won the war of independence. The Jordanians and the Lebanese had already signed ceasefire agreements. The Syrians had yet to sign one, but had stopped fighting. The Egyptians had made a second attempt to recapture the Negev, but were soundly defeated.

We had done the impossible. They had come at us from all sides, those armies of seven neighboring Arab countries -- Egypt, the Sudan, Saudi Arabia, Transjordan, Iraq, Syria, and Lebanon; and they added their power to that of our next-door neighbors, the

Palestinians, who fought us in our own backyard; and we clung with our nails and teeth to every rock and every blade of grass, and we bled on every turn of the road and on every field, and we won.

And the words of the poet, Shin Shalom, came to mind:

> *Shehecheyanu...*
> *Who kept us in life, and preserved us, and enabled us to reach this day,*
> *For I am not dreaming, nor am I having a vision,*
> *For it is all true.*

If 1948 was the year of the war, 1949 was the year of the actual birth of the new state. Officially, Israel was born on November 29, 1947, the night the United Nations in Flushing Meadows, New York, voted by two-thirds majority to divide Palestine between Arabs and Jews. The actual Jewish state was born on May 14, 1948, at the museum in Tel Aviv, where David Ben-Gurion read the Declaration of Independence. For the next nine months, the midwives delivering the newly born state were we, the men and women and even the children of the Yishuv, of the towns and villages of the Galilee, the Coast, the Valley, the Judean Hills and the Negev desert.

Those were a grim nine months, and I have always remembered them in shades of gray, never in color. It was as though the sun never shone during that time. The grass did not grow, the flowers did not bloom. The little color I do remember from those days is the orange rind of that solitary sample of the national Israeli fruit my mother gave me one morning when I went to school, and said, "Make it last the whole day. It's the only food you are going to have today. I have nothing else to give you." The color red was on people's mind for only one reason, a reason colored by fear and pain and bereavement. And then a bright white color flashes through my mind, like a glimmer of hope among the shades of gray. It is the color of a wedding gown. It is the marriage of my cousin Genia from France, to Jean, a graduate of the French Resistance who had come to fight in his people's struggle for independence. More about Jean and Genia later.

Out of those shades of gray was born 1949, the year during which the actual birth of the state took place. Until that point the question was hanging in the air -- will a birth actually take place? Could the war against all those enemies be won? Did a few hundred thousand Jews in a land dominated for centuries by foreign powers have the wherewithal to establish a viable state which was going to last, have the means and the power to resist new attempts by its neighbors, be able to feed its starving people, and, most important, be able to absorb the hundreds of thousands and possibly millions of Jews from all parts of the world who waited to come, who had nowhere else to go, and for whose sake, in the final analysis, this most unusual of states was created?

And so 1949, a year not nearly as romantic as its predecessors -- 1947 and 1948, was truly the most critical of them all. It was the year of the actual birth, the year when the new state started breathing, showing the first signs of life, making its first moves.

The guns were finally silent. There was much mourning going on. There was hardly a family in Israel that didn't lose someone in this war. The songs mourning the dead were on everyone's lips. *B'arvot Ha'negev*, In the Wilderness of the Negev, *Bahb el Wahd*, the Gate to the Valley, were perhaps the two best known.

They were sung over and over again, never to the end, for somewhere in the middle of the song one's throat began to choke and the tears burst out. The poet, Haim Guri, gave expression to what we all felt when he wrote,

Behold, our bodies are lying still - a long, long row.
Our faces are altered - death stares from our eyes, we do not
breathe.
The last light is extinguished, and evening descends on the
hills.
Behold, we will not rise to walk in the fields in the glow of
a distant sunset.
We will not love, we will not pluck gentle, hushed
strings.
We will not shout in the gardens when the wind whistles
through the trees.

And another great poet of that period, Natan Alterman, added:

We are the silver platter
Upon which the Jewish State
Was delivered.

There was bereavement everywhere, but the newly born, the state itself, was alive and breathing. The miracle had come to pass, and even a ten-year-old child understood the magnitude of that miracle.

It was time to start living, start exploring, make plans, ask questions about the future. One of my greatest desires at that time was to go out and see the world. Until that time I had never

149

travelled more than a few miles from my home town. I told my mother I wanted to go somewhere and start expanding my horizons. I was sure she was going to try to talk me out of it, but to my surprise she was in full sympathy. She suggested I go to visit our relatives in Tel Aviv.

The coast from Haifa to Tel Aviv was now safe for travel, and my parents gave me permission to travel by myself on a Sherut -- a cab service consisting of large commodious Chryslers or De Sotos in which two folding seats were installed between the front and the back seats by the new Yellow Checkered Cab company which transported up to seven passengers on each run. That trip to Tel Aviv has remained vivid in my mind to this day, although nothing extraordinary happened. I simply went to visit my father's cousin, Menachem, who lived in Tel Aviv with his wife, Tova, and their one-year-old son, Haim.

The war had just ended, and the songs, poems and stories of the war began to appear in print. I recall taking along on the trip several books to read, which included a collection of Palmach songs by Haim Hefer, which have since become Israeli classics. I knew every word of that book by heart, but seeing them in print . gave me a sense of being part of history. They were *my* songs, and they expressed the feelings of everyone around me. I also took along a book which had just come off the press, called *In the Fields of Philistia* by Uri Avneri, a diary of a young soldier fighting in the Negev. It was a beautiful and stirring account of the war, and a runaway best-seller in Israel in those days. Its author would become one of Israel's leading and most controversial journalists, and an advocate of an accommodation with the PLO, which has since become a reality.

Another book I recall taking along with me was called *1984* by an English writer named George Orwell. It was a very strange futuristic political fantasy about a very scary new world. What I didn't realize at the time was that Orwell was talking about 1948, not 1984, and that the world he described was taking shape in Eastern Europe, under Bolshevism.

And, finally, I borrowed one of my mother's romances, the title of which I no longer recall. It was about poverty-stricken German brother and sister during Hitler's rise to power. In their desperate search for love and happiness they end up making love to each other, at which point their mother, crazed with despair, shoots both of them.

I remember exploring Tel Aviv on Menachem's big heavy bicycle. And I also remember taking a walk on the *Tayelet,* the Tel Aviv beach, with Tova, who pushed Haim in his baby carriage. In a picture we took together having ice cream in one of Tel Aviv's famous cafes across from the beach, I am wearing my khaki shirt and pants and my sandals, my hair straight and blond, and as I study this ten-year-old boy in the picture I find it hard to believe he was reading all those books on that weekend in Tel Aviv.

Perhaps the reason I remember this particular trip so well -- and I had taken many more exciting trips shortly thereafter -- is because it marked the end of the beginning. The war was over. Life was starting. The dream was now a reality.

PART II:

THE LAND

39.

The birth was over. The smoke had cleared over the battlefields as the guns fell silent. The land wore deep birthmarks everywhere. There were buildings poked with bullet holes in all parts of Haifa, in frontier kibbutzim like Negba and Ramat Rah'hel and Yad Mordechai, and in strongholds like Nebi Yusha and Iraq Sueidan and Auja Al Hafir. There were abandoned Arab homes in towns from Tiberias to Beer Sheba, and many an abandoned Arab village. The great human tragedy of the Palestinian Arab refugees had started, and the great human drama of a new nation of Jews born out of the ashes of the Holocaust and the world-wide centuries-old dispersion was unfolding. It was 1949, and I was ten. As I mentioned before, I do not recall the age of ten as being particularly glamorous. To me -- as to most ten year olds -- it was a transition period, from childhood to puberty and adolescence. It was an awkward time of my life, but I was deeply aware of the profound change that was taking place all around me. The romantic period of the birth of the state and the war of liberation was over. The soldiers, including my father, took off their uniform and came home to face the daily reality of life in an infant state that was just beginning to learn how to walk and talk. The many problems that had been put on hold for the past year and a half now had to be met head on. Shiploads and planeloads of new, poor immigrants kept arriving every day, ill-equipped to deal with life in this new land. Many of them were emotionally scarred from the horrors of the war in Europe. Others came from cultures radically different from ours, from countries like Aden and Afghanistan and the Atlas Mountains in North Africa. Some had never in their lives eaten with a fork and knife, or sat at a table. Nearly all of them had to be housed and fed, be given job training, taught Hebrew, and helped along in

153

making the transition from refugees and immigrants to citizens of this new country called Israel.

And, at the same time, the new state had to invent all the things a state needs -- currency, stamps, civil service, a form of government, laws and law enforcement, emissaries to other lands, and on and on. I don't envy the work schedule our leaders -- Ben-Gurion, Golda Meir, Moshe Sharett, and all the rest -- had to face that year. How they did it is beyond me. They must have hardly slept that year. But somehow they managed. Somehow all of us managed. We -- young and adult -- were called upon that year and during the next several years to make many sacrifices -- make do without many basic necessities and perform a great deal of volunteer work to help the newly born state become alive and well. We were told that although our neighboring Arab countries had signed cease-fire agreements with us, the war was far from over. Right now, the main battle was not against invading Arab armies, but against all the social and economic problems besieging us and threatening our existence. In a way, we were like the Russians after the Bolshevik Revolution, when they started their five-year plans and were called upon over and over again by their leaders to sacrifice for a better future. The difference between us and the Russian people was that they had to do those things under coercion, which in the end did not work out, while we did it because we wanted to, and because we realized we had no other choice.

And I recall how we -- both young and adult -- did a great deal of complaining and grumbling, not unlike the Children of Israel in the wilderness after the exodus, and felt sorry for ourselves having to go through so much hardship. But we did not give up. We did what we had to do.

154

In the second half of this book I would like to take a look at what it was like to live during the aftermath of the birth, both as the observant child I was in those days, and in retrospect. Looking back, it was a very critical time. The newly born state could have easily died in its infancy, as many so-called experts around the world actually believed it might, and as many of our neighbors sincerely hoped it would. Certainly the world did not stand at the cradle of the newly born and offered all sorts of help. Quite the contrary. Hillel's dictum, "If I am not for myself who is for me?" was true in regard to us in full measure. No, 1949 was not a romantic time. Nor were 1950 or the years that followed. But out of the strain and conflicts and the grinding reality of that period a viable country was born. Let's revisit that time and see what it was like.

40

The arrival of thousands of Holocaust survivors during and after the birth of the state forced us, the new Israelis, to confront the question of the Holocaust. The timing of the Holocaust was very strange to a young boy living in Haifa at that time. Here we were, taught about Jewish heroics dating back to Samson and Judah Maccabee and more recent mythologized characters like Joseph Trumpeldor and Aharon Aharonson. We were the next generation of soldiers who would be trained to take on anyone. And at the same time, our relatives were being led like sheep to the slaughter in Europe, offering little resistance, and treated like so much human garbage. Clearly, we of the Yishuv in the Land of Israel and our counterparts in Europe were on totally different wave lengths. Our agendas were totally different as well. They were trying to catch another breath of air, live another day, and hope to survive. We were redeeming another dunham of land, planting another tree, smuggling in another gun, and assembling the future army of Israel, man by man, rifle by rifle, hand grenade by hand grenade.

It was a most unusual time. And, as a result, I, in my little world in Haifa, had very strange ideas about what had just taken place in Europe.

In 1948, the most horrible war ever waged in all of human history had been over for three years. But the devastation was so great that Europe was still reeling from what took place during the six prior years. There were still refugees roaming the highways and byways of Europe, there was a new monster in Europe known as Russian communism, which, in the name of human love and brotherhood began to swallow up countries and expand the atrocities of Joseph Djugashvili Stalin as far as Yugoslavia and Hungary. There was terrible hunger and poverty in Italy, of which we children in Haifa got a small glimpse through the black and white movies of directors like Vittorio de Sica, notably "The Bitter Rice," "The Bicycle Thieves," "Rome an Open City," and so on. And finally, and most palpably, the Jewish Holocaust survivors began to arrive in Haifa. They were not received with open arms.

Yes, it pains me to say it, almost fifty years later, but it's true. We children didn't quite know what to make of them. They were skeletal, they wore strange clothes which did not fit them, they let off strange odors. They were not the kind of people we were used to identify as Jews. Our kind of Jews smelled of the open air, the fields, the sun, and the sea. We wore simple utilitarian clothes, and we did not look at every corner fearing a lurking danger, although there were plenty of dangers around. And so we didn't quite know what to make of our newly founds "uncles" and "aunts."

And, looking back, although no one would admit it, they were an embarrassment to us. We were preparing for the great showdown, the birth of the state, the war that would follow, the creation of a new nation. Our elders did not wish us, the young, to receive mixed messages. They did not want us to know that a Jew could mean a lot of different things, and, worst of all, that Jews could be treated the way they were treated in Europe during World War Two.

And then there was another problem, by no means easier than those previous ones, and, in effect, much worse. When the war ended my parents and their friends were hoping against hope that at least some of their loved ones -- a mother, a father, a brother or a sister, might have survived the Shoah. People spent hours looking through newspapers for names, writing letters to all sorts of organizations and governmental bodies, discussing the

157

matter among themselves, and so on. Even as a little boy I clearly remember those discussions that went on for months and years. By 1948 those impossible hopes began to evaporate. People stopped searching, their hopes dashed against the grim reality that began to sink in -- their loved ones were all gone forever. None had survived.

It was around that time that the surviving remnants began to arrive. I don't know how it all started, but soon rumors started to fly -- those who survived were mainly the ones who took advantage of others, who snatched a piece of bread from the mouth of a dying person, and, worse yet, who collaborated with the Germans. On the streets of Haifa in 1948 it was a common sight for a Holocaust survivor to stop in the middle of the street, point at another person, and shout, "I recognize this person! He was a kapo in my camp! He killed my brother!"

No doubt some of those allegations were true. But the bad thing was they were blown out of proportion, and soon everyone became suspect. And, I imagine, subconsciously, many of our parents chose to believe that among those who were now arriving from Europe was someone who somehow was responsible for the fact that one's mother, or uncle, or grandparents did not survive the war.

Looking back I must say it was very unfair to the survivors, painting them with that same broad brush which should have been reserved for only a few. Having studied the Holocaust for the past forty years, I can say that each survivor has his or her own story of how and why they survived, and many survived not because they took advantage of others but because they were resourceful, or lucky, or both. But all of this, of course, is hindsight.

Among the survivors I remember from those days was a

young couple, who stopped in our house, and had dinner with us. I remember them telling me some stories about what happened to them during the war. They were both partisans. They hid in the woods. They attacked German patrols and trains. They were thin and wiry, but I remember how they showed me their muscles. Both the man and the woman had bulging muscles when they rolled up their sleeves, clenched their fists and brought them tight against their chests. It made an impression on me as a child who was just starting to develop his own muscles. I was very happy to know there were also Jews in Europe who had muscles and guts and fought back.

Which brings me to Moteleh, one of those survivors who arrived in 1948. He happened to be a second cousin of my mother's, and to me he symbolizes the entire Holocaust. Moteleh. I can still see him, so many years later. Really, a pathetic character, a proverbial Jewish shlemazel. Emaciated, always with a dark stubble, sunken cheeks, his Adam's apple always working. It's now 1949, and Moteleh has been drafted into the newly formed Israeli army. He works in the quartermaster unit. He has some kind of duties in the kitchen in a British army base outside Haifa, now an Israeli base. Near Bat Galim. Whenever he is on leave he comes to our home, and he brings my mother some luxury items, such as chocolate, or ground coffee, which are rationed, and which we can scarcely obtain. She pays him nicely for those items, and it helps him improve his standard of living somewhat.

Moteleh. He wears the new dark olive green khaki uniform of the Israeli army, two sizes too large, and a beret of the same color, and he looks like the comical Czech character, the Good Soldier Schweik, of Czech fame. Some of his teeth are gold crowned. He hardly ever smiles, but when he does, his teeth shine.

Moteleh. He did not lose his faith in God during his years in Auschwitz (now that I think of it, I fail to understand how a weak creature like Moteleh survived Auschwitz in the first place). He is still a religious Jew. For him, God did not die in the Holocaust, like it did for Elie Wiesel. I knew Elie before he became famous. I went to visit him once in his little apartment on the west side of Manhattan. I told him, "Elie, in your book *Night* you say that you saw God die in Auschwitz. This is twenty years later, Elie. Do you still believe God died in Auschwitz?"

Wiesel gave me a pained look. He said to me after a short

pause: "Maimonides says, some questions only have one answer
-- silence."

Moteleh was not nearly as clever as Elie Wiesel, perhaps the
most famous survivor of Auschwitz. He was just an ordinary
Jew. The most ordinary of ordinary Jews. He took me to
services at a small synagogue off Arlozoroff Street in Haifa. I
really liked it. My parents never took me to services. I was very
intrigued by this whole business of God and praying to God and
so on. My parents did not pray to God. They had left God in
Europe when they became pioneers and went to rebuild the land
of Israel. But as a child I liked the idea of praying to God. It
gave life an added dimension. It sort of made sense out of the
whole business of why I was born, and why all that struggle was
going on. Besides, as a second grader I had started to learn the
Bible. "In the beginning God created the heaven and the earth."
I was glad there was someone who started this whole thing.
Otherwise, how is one to explain where it all came from, and
where it was all going to?

So he took me to services one morning. I believe it was the
morning of Shavuot, the harvest holiday. And afterwards he
talked to me about that prayer they pronounced at the service,
"Shehecheyanu..." It gave thanks to God for having kept us
alive, and preserved us, and brought us to this joyous occasion.

I thought it was a rather nice prayer. Moteleh, however,
looked at me with deep sadness in his eyes. He shook his head,
as if trying to decide whether he could share his innermost
feelings with an eight year old. After hesitating for a while, he
said,

"You are young, you may not understand. And, besides,
you were not there. Those who were not there cannot
understand. No one here does. But you are a smart child, and I

161

like you, so I will tell you what I think. We say this prayer, and we thank God for having preserved us, and kept us alive. But God really didn't. He didn't preserve his own people, He let us die like flies. God forgive me for saying this, but this prayer is not true."

I hardly understood what Moteleh was talking about. But I could feel his pain. And I knew then and there something terrible had happened. And it put a sadness in my heart that has been there ever since. And will always be there.

A year later Moteleh was released from the army. He moved to Petah Tikva. Another year passed and we received an invitation to his wedding. A week before the wedding my father found a short news item in the morning newspaper. "Mordecai Abrabanel, a fireman in Petah Tikva, died in a house fire trying to save a child."

42.

Jews in Haifa in 1949 came from every corner of the world. We called it the "ingathering of the exiles." We were taught in school that for two thousand years Jews were scattered throughout the world. They lived in almost every country on earth, spoke every language imaginable, took on many of the customs of every culture, including music, food, habits, mannerisms, and so on. But no matter how far they roamed, or how isolated they were from the rest of the world, in places like Yemen or Ethiopia, they all -- in the words of the Psalmist -- remembered Zion.

> *By the rivers of Babylon there we sat, yeah, we wept*
> *When we remembered Zion.*
> *We hung our harps upon the willows in the midst of it,*
> *For our captors asked us to sing the songs of Zion.*
> *How can we sing the songs of Zion in a strange land?*
> *If I forget thee, O Jerusalem, may my right hand forget*
> * its cunning,*
> *May my tongue become fused to my palate if I remember*
> *You not, if I do not put Jerusalem above my chiefest joy.*

I know that all people love their homeland. But to judge from the above Psalm, did any people ever love their homeland more than we Jews have loved the land of Israel? I don't think so. We were gone for centuries, but we never forgot her. Or, at least, some of us in every generation and in every land never forgot. We call those who remembered the "saving remnant." What is truly amazing, is the fact that a Jew from Yemen or a Jew from Germany or a Jew from Peru can feel just as intensely about her. The fact is, when an Italian, for instance, leaves Italy (and Italy in my opinion is one of the most lovable countries in the

163

world), and immigrates to a country like Argentina, or Mexico, or the United States, it is almost a given that his children and grandchildren will become Argentinians or Mexicans or Americans with only a fond memory of the old country. Not so the Jews. We can be very loyal citizens of Argentina or Mexico or the United States. But in our hearts burns the love of Zion, and the word "Jerusalem" makes our heart tremble and our soul ache.

I first went to Jerusalem in the fall of 1949, with my cousin Genia from France, and her husband, Jean. As I recall, it was a very emotional experience. What was particularly emotional about it was the fact that the holy places I had learned about in school -- the Western Wall, the Temple Mount, David's Tower, Rachel's Tomb, to mention only a few, had all been occupied by Jordan, or Transjordan, as it was called in those days, and barbed wire fences cut through the heart of Jerusalem, preventing me from seeing any of those places. I could only get a glimpse of the Old City by going up the tall tower of the Jerusalem YMCA, across the street from the King David Hotel. Somewhere amid the narrow streets of the Suq of the Old City was the Wailing Wall, but you couldn't see it. You could only dream about it, just as Jews in exile dreamed about it for two thousand years. Looking back, it was quite an irony. We had just won our war of liberation, but we had been cut off from our holiest places. Clearly, something was wrong, and someday it had to be rectified, and one day it was.

But coming back to the "ingathering of the exiles." For hundreds of years Jews in different countries and even in different regions of the same country had very little contact with one another. In Poland, for example, Jews in southeastern Poland were known as Galician Jews, *Galitzianers* in Yiddish. Jews in northeastern Poland were known as *Litvaks*, or Lithuanian Jews. Jews from the capital city, Warsaw, were known as *Varshavers*, and Jews from western Poland were borderline *Yekkes*, or German Jews. The late prime minister of Israel, Menachem Begin, once told me when we spent a weekend together in Cleveland, Ohio, that he and his wife, Aliza, were a mixed marriage. What he meant was, albeit tongue in cheek, he was a *Litvak*, and his wife a *Galitzianer*. Behind the humor was a very clear-cut fact of life, which I experienced vividly during my childhood. Jews from the Galician part of Poland did not trust Jews from the Lithuanian part of Poland, and vice versa. Galician Jews were accused by the Lithuanians of being too emotional, ill-mannered, and devious in their business practices. The Hasidic movement, which emphasized the emotional side of religion, flourished in Galicia, but had a hard time in Lithuania. The Galician Jews, for their part, looked upon the *Litvaks* as cold and overly rational, straight-laced and all but naive. The latter made fun of the Yiddish accent of the former, and vice versa. As a general rule, *Galitzianers* preferred to marry *Galitzianers*, and ditto for all the other groups. No wonder Begin, who was known to be the most loving and devoted of husbands, nonetheless felt impelled to make this quip about his own marriage after he asked me where my parents were from, and I told him from Galicia.

Yes, in Haifa in 1949 we all made fun of every other group except our own. This practice must go back in time to the dawn of human life, perhaps to the time of the caveman. Indeed, Haifa has been determined to be the home of one of the early versions of the caveman, remains of whom were found in the caves on Mount Carmel. But my recollections only go back to the time of the birth of the state, so I will refrain from discussing caveman humor.

The sequence of the Jewish ethnic evolution in Haifa goes somewhat like this:

The first pioneers in the beginning of the century came from Russia. Along came a smattering of Jews from Arab countries. This gave rise to the dichotomy of *Ashkenazim* -- European Jews, and *Sephardim* -- Jews from the lands of Islam, also referred to as Oriental Jews. For many years this dichotomy would persist, and not until recent years have the barriers between "European" and "Oriental" Jews started to come down. I might add that the term *Sephardim* covers a very wide gamut of Jewish ethnic groups. At one end of the spectrum we find the small group of authentic Sephardim, namely, Jews whose ancestors actually came from *Sepharad*, Hebrew for Spain. They left Spain in 1492, expelled by the not-so-enlightened Catholic rulers of this tragic country, and settled in countries around the Mediterranean (later also in Holland, England, and the United States). Some of them settled in the Holy Land, where they lived when the early 20th century pioneers began to arrive from Russia. They were the true aristocracy of the early yishuv in the Land of Israel. No one made fun of them, since they were refined and well-off, while the pioneers were coarse and poor. They were the proud remnant of one of the most glorious Jewries in the history of the world, namely, Spanish Jewry, personified by the great Moses ben Maimon, or Maimonides, of whom it was said, "From Moses [of biblical fame] to Moses [Maimonides] there has been none like Moses," which is true, considering the fact that no one has had a greater impact on Jewish thought and religious practice than Maimonides (not to mention his impact on Christian theology and on medicine). Besides Maimonides, they gave us the greatest Hebrew poet since biblical times, Yehudah Halevi (who sang, "I live in the West, but my heart is in the east... O Zion, won't you inquire about the welfare of your captives?"), and other great men and women in every field. My mother's grandmother's maiden name was Abrabanel, the name of the finance minister of Ferdinand and Isabella, the Catholic Kings of Spain who expelled the Jews in 1492. Abrabanel was a family of great financiers as well as great Torah scholars and commentators. According to my mother, her grandmother had a family tree (which disappeared in the Holocaust), tracing the family all the way back to the 15th century Abrabanel family in Spain. I recall how proud I felt as a child when I learned in my Jewish history class that the Spanish Abrabanels traced their lineage all the way back to King David.

At the other end of the Sphardic spectrum were very poor Jews from neighboring Arab and Muslim countries who migrated to Palestine. They came from places like Horan, Buchara, Aden, Yemen, and other far corners of Asia and Africa. Some of them worked at the hardest menial jobs at Haifa Harbor. They were so poor and unworldly, that they gave rise to some expressions which found their way into the reborn Hebrew vernacular, such as "*Anah Horani*," or, "*Anah Kurdi*." (literally, I am from Horan, or, I am from Kurdistan). It was a way of saying, "I don't know a thing," or, "I am illiterate."

Between these two extremes were all the other Sephardic or Oriental Jews, who came from nearly all the lands of Islam, from Morocco in the west to India in the east. More about them in a minute.

In the late 20s and early 30s Jews began to arrive from Poland, one of the largest Jewish communities in the world at that time. Among them were a young man and a young woman who eight years later would become my parents. Polish Jews, especially the ones from southeastern Poland, a region known in

167

those days as Galicia, were great joke-tellers. It is not so hard to figure out why. First, most of them were quite poor in those many towns and villages of Poland, yet nearly all of them were literate, and many of them were quite learned, and humor is one way the educated poor can deal with poverty. Secondly, they had neither radio nor television nor spectator sports in those days, and one way to pass the time was by telling jokes. And last but not least, they were very provincial people, who lived and died within a small area of a few square miles, and anyone from any distance at all was a stranger to them, therefore the object of suspicion and jokes.

And so these Galician Jews made fun of everyone, and, in return, everyone made fun of them. Everyone in those days played "Jewish geography," a game designed to find out where your parents were from, and how one was to treat you. Grownups would say to me something like this:

"Do I know your parents?"

"I'm not sure."

"Where did they come from in Europe?" (My Slavic features and light hair made it abundantly clear my parents were from Europe, not from the lands of Islam).

"Poland."

"Oh! Which part of Poland?"

"Galicia."

Here a familiar expression would come over my investigator's face. It would be a mixture of a derisive smile and commiseration, as if to say, "We can't choose our parents, can we?"

"Ah! *Galitzianers!*" the person would say, nodding his or her head in feigned sympathy.

As a small child I once asked my mother why people got that

expression on their face when I told them where she and father were from. I also asked her if it was true that all *Galitzianers* were crafty, shifty, not to be trusted. She explained to me that Jews from other parts of Poland and Europe were jealous of the Jews of Galicia, because they were very clever people, and no one could put anything over on them. Even then I recall thinking that the coin had two sides. One person's "clever" was another person's "crafty," or "shifty." There was something about ianers which, I must admit, was not very endearing, as there is about every group, I suppose. We tend to see other people's faults more easily than we see our own, and so we joke about them more than we joke about ourselves. But I must add that Jews in general are very good at poking fun at themselves. We don't take ourselves nearly so seriously as some people think we do. Witness the old Jewish observation, "Oh God, why didn't You choose someone else?"

The Russian pioneers were mostly socialists, one might say Marxist Zionists (which sounds to me like somewhat of an oxymoron), who sought to implement the teachings of Marx within a Zionist context in the Middle East, and serve as a model for humanity in realizing the ideals first enunciated by the French Revolution (*Liberté, Égalité, Fraternité*), as understood by Karl Marx and by the founders of Zionist Socialism -- men like Ber Borochov, A. D. Gordon, Berl Katzenelson, and so on. The Polish Zionists were more "bourgeois," and many of them belonged to either moderate, non-socialist Zionist organizations such as the General Zionists, or to right-wing nationalistic Zionist organizations, notably the Revisionist Zionists, which in time would become the Likud party in present-day Israel. As a result, the Russian pioneers turned to agriculture, and founded the kibbutzim, kvutzot, and moshavim, or to industry, and started the

169

great labor union, the Histadrut. The Polish pioneers for the most part -- my parents included -- settled in urban areas like Tel Aviv and Haifa, and took a leading part in starting what would become the new middle class. Consequently, the Russians would often look suspiciously on the Poles, considering them less than true Zionists, since they, the Russians, believed that socialist Zionism was the only true way, while General Zionism was a watered down version, and Revisionist Zionism was a downright traitor of the true ideals of the movement as they understood it. I don't, however, recall (and here I may be challenged, because, admittedly, I am speaking from a purely personal perspective) too many jokes told in those days by the Russians about us Poles. Those Russian Jews were more interested in pioneering and political activism than humor. There is no questioning their preeminence in the creation of the State of Israel. After all, they are the ones who gave us Bialik, Jabotinsky, Ahad Haam, Chaim Weitzmann, Golda Meir, and Ben-Gurion, in a word, most of the top thinkers and leaders of Zionism and Israel. But, come to think of it, I don't recall either Ben-Gurion or Golda Meir, certainly not Ahad Haam or Jabotinsky, having a particularly good sense of humor. Nor Begin, for that matter. Although, I must admit, Bialik had a great sense of humor, which I suspect was more Galician than Russian, given Bialik's origins which were somewhat of a mix.

The real fun began when the German Jews began to arrive in the late 30s. As I mentioned earlier, this was a rather unusual group of German Jews. It included some great scholars and scientists, educators and financiers, who were forced to leave Germany because of the Nazi party rise to power in 1933. Many of them preferred Haifa to, say, Tel Aviv, since Haifa is a mountain city, thus cooler than Tel Aviv, which lies on the flat

170

warm coast of the Mediterranean, and since Haifa is more similar climactically and topographically to Germany. Soon they were accorded a nickname -- *Yekkes*, which stuck almost to this day. Where exactly did that name come from? There does not seem to be any clear and convincing answer to this question. Over the years I have heard two. The first, which dates back to my childhood, maintains that the word is an acronym, consisting of the Hebrew letter YKH (the way the word is actually spelled in Hebrew). These letters are purported to stand for the words *Yehudi Keshe Havanah*, which means, a Jew of slow understanding. According to this stereotype, the German Jew, while highly educated, lacked common sense, and was not at home in the wily ways of the Middle East. Years later, in fact only recently, I heard a more convincing explanation. The word *Yekke* is a derivation of the European word "jacket." The German Jews who arrived in Haifa in the late 30s surprised the khaki-clad, informal pioneers as he strolled on Herzl and Nordau Streets wearing a jacket and a necktie, even in the hottest days of the summer, and the word jacket became *Yekke*.

Back in Europe, German and Polish Jews have had a long history of mutual disdain. Polish Jews who migrated to Germany were looked down upon by native German Jews, who considered their cousins from the East, to whom they referred as *Ost Juden* (Eastern Jews), uncouth and unsophisticated, indeed an embarrassment to them, the cultivated and refined *Deutsche Juden*. The Polish Jews, in turn, considered the German Jews pseudo-German assimilationists, self-hating Jews who tried to pass for Gentiles. So when German Jews began to arrive in Haifa, the love-hate relationship between them and the Polish Jews blossomed, and gave rise to a rich repertoire of humor. The originators of the jokes were mainly the Polish Jews, who

171

undoubtedly were jealous of their much better educated and more sophisticated German counterparts and felt the need to stereotype them and cut them down to size. One of my favorites is the following joke, told to me by my mother:

> A German Jew back in the old country went to the market to sell a cow. He stood in the middle of the market next to his cow and waited for customers to make him an offer. As people stopped by to inquire about the cow, the owner explained that the cow gave milk in moderation. Naturally, no one wanted to buy the cow. A *Galitzianer* happened by and saw the *Yekke* looking glum. He asked him what's wrong, and the *Yekke* explained he was unable to sell his cow. "Don't worry," the Galitzianer reassured him, "let me sell your cow. You will see how fast I'll sell it." The *Yekke* agreed, and stepped aside. The *Galitzianer* stood in front of the cow and started to call out in a loud voice, "Gather one, gather all, here is the best milking cow this side of Breslau! Don't miss your chance!" Sure enough, in less than five minutes the cow was sold. When the *Galitzianer* turned to the *Yekke* and handed him his money, he noticed that the *Yekke* was still looking glum. "What's the matter?" he asked him, "didn't I sell your cow?" "Yes, you did," the *Yekke* responded. "But had I known this cow gave so much milk I wouldn't have sold it!"

After the birth of the state we received a large immigration of Romanian Jews. They spoke Yiddish quite like Polish Jews, and in many ways were very similar to their Polish cousins. Many of them, I recall, were housed in the Lower City of Haifa, in old stone residential buildings once occupied by our Arab neighbors.

172

It seems to me that they became acclimated quickly in our midst, and fit quite well into the Jewish community of the new Israeli Haifa. They did, however, manage to acquire a rather unpleasant reputation for being less than honest, in fact, the common derogatory Yiddish expression appended to them was *Rumeinische goniff,* or Romanian thief. Certainly, they were not all thieves. But whether or not they had a disproportionate number of thieves among them, the title took hold, and never seemed to have completely disappeared. Jokes about the "Romanian thieves" could fill up a volume. The one that sticks out in my mind is the following:

> A plane flew from Sweden to Israel. Half way there, one passenger asked his neighbor, "Excuse me, what time is it?" The second gentleman looked at his wrist and cried, "My watch is gone!" Soon many passengers could be heard saying to one another, "So is mine, so is mine!" As everyone looked at his neighbors in disbelief, the pilot's voice was heard, "Sorry, we forgot to make the announcement. We are now flying over Romanian air space, and all passengers are asked to watch their personal belongings!"

So we all made fun of one another. And we loved jokes, as all Jews do. We could never have enough of them. At a young age I started to collect joke books. Naturally, they were full of Jewish ethnic jokes, and jokes about Jews and Gentiles, and Jews and Arabs, and you name it. We even had jokes from China and Australia and Tierra del Fuego, which must have undergone serious transformations by the time they reached us. But for some reason unknown to me, we had a place of honor for jokes

173

about the people of Scotland. According to popular belief, the Scottish people were perceived as extremely stingy, and their stinginess gave rise to an endless stream of jokes. To conclude this chapter, I will tell one:

A plane flies over Glasgow. The passengers notice that the lights in the houses down below keep going on and off. They ask the flight attendant for the reason. "Oh," says the affable young man, "there must be a lot of Scotch people down there reading books. Every time they turn a page they turn off the light to save electricity."

43.

The adults in Haifa at that time told many stories about their life in the shtetl, the little village or town of Eastern Europe, where they grew up. Those stories became part of my childhood dreamworld. It was a faraway land called Polania, Hebrew for Poland. It was very different from the Mediterranean seaport where I grew up. Polania had a long cold winter with snow and ice and frozen lakes and rivers, and short summers with few days of sunshine. It also had deep forests where one could get lost and run into wolves and bears. And on the edge of those woods, on the bank of a river or a lake, was that mythical little town called the shtetl. In its little wooden houses lived my grandparents and uncles and aunts, and also my father and mother when they were very young. Outside the shtetl was the estate where the Poritz, the lord of the manor, who owned the fields and forests around the shtetl, lived and held court. Nearby lived the Polish and Ukrainian farmers, who were not particularly fond of Jews.

I knew, of course, that the shtetl was gone, consumed by the hatred and brutality of the Second World War. But its memory was so vivid in the minds of people around me, that I could almost touch its presence. It lived on in the hearts and minds of my parents and their friends, and shaped their feelings and actions. Sometimes I felt as though I myself was living in the shtetl, where my ancestors lived for centuries. Haifa was only an accidental place, a shore against which I happened to be tossed one day by accident. The real place was the shtetl, where my soul, my mind, my imagination, my customs and traditions, everything that made up my personal reality, belonged. I lived in a place I had never seen, which nonetheless was more real than anything around me. I was only a leaf on a tree, but the tree was old and mighty, and had deep roots. The trunk and the roots of that tree were planted in the soil of Polania, and my soul yearned for that tree. This is why, as a child, I was so fond of the stories and tales of the writers of the shtetl, Sholem Asch and Yod Lamed Peretz and Sholem Aleichem and the brothers Singer, only to mention a few. I yearned for the trunk and the roots. I yearned for all those members of my mother's and father's families I never knew, and will never know, but whose presence was more real to me than anything in this breathing world.

We tend to romanticize the past, especially the past of our own family and our own people. We tend to forget the bad experiences, and only remember the good. Surely there was much in shtetl life that was good and enduring. After all, this life did last for centuries. There was family closeness and cohesion. There was the pure, innocent faith in a good God who some day will send his messiah and redeem his people. There was a wondrous movement called Hasidism, founded two hundred years ago by the great Rabbi Israel, the Baal Shem Tov, He of the Good Name. Hasidism taught its millions of adherents in Eastern Europe how to sing and dance with great fervor and in total devotion to the Almighty. It elevated the poor, downtrodden Jew into a higher spiritual world where he became a child of God, a member of the heavenly hosts. It taught goodness and kindness and decency. It gave its followers strong, lasting hope.

But the messiah never came to the shtetl. Instead, the most evil and monstrous of all the human manifestations of evil this earth has ever known came one day and used every imaginable and unimaginable method to kill millions of men, women and children and put an end forever to the life of the shtetl.

Indeed, the recently completed Holocaust Museum in Washington, DC, I am told, has its central lobby, several stories high, completely covered with old photographs of the men, women and children of one such shtetl, whose place of burial is

176

unknown, since they were never accorded a proper burial, entire families done unto death without a single survivor, whose only memorial is this exhibit which represents thousands of such towns and villages where millions of Jews waited for the messiah for so long.

For me and my generation growing up in what would become the Jewish state this belief in a messiah became something else. Our fathers and mothers never talked to us about any messiah. They left the messiah in Europe when they came to this land, and, who knows? Perhaps he is still there. And perhaps he had died at Auschwitz. They taught us something altogether different. They taught us that redemption is not achieved through supernatural means, but through human actions. Every year on Hanukkah we sang:

> *We carry torches*
> *Through dark nights.*
> *The ground burns under our feet*
> *And anyone whose heart yearn for the light*
> *May lift his eyes to us*
> *And come along!*
> *A miracle did not happen to us,*
> *We did not find a cruse of oil.*
> *We drilled all the way through the granite,*
> *And behold, there was light!*

I suppose we ourselves were the messiah. We made the miracle happen. But it all started in those little villages and towns in Eastern Europe known as the Shtetl, where our parents dreamed of the promised land, and made the dream a reality. And so the shtetl lives forever in the hearts of their children,

177

immortalized in story and play and song, in *Fiddler on the Roof* and *Tevye the Milkman*, in *Oifen pripichik* and *Mein yiddishe mammeh* and *Mein shteteleh Belz*, and in the tales of the Hasidim. To use the words of the national Hebrew poet, Bialik, the shtetl was the shop where the soul of the nation was fashioned.

44.

Unlike many of my schoolmates in grade school, who preferred modern subjects such as math or social studies, I was particularly fond of the Bible. Biblical heroes held a fascination for me from the day I could think in sentences. It grew when I started school at age six, and kept growing all the time, and still does. First there were, of course, Moses and Mordecai and the patriarchs and matriarchs, whom I knew from such holidays as Passover and Purim. And there were also post-biblical heroes, like Judah Maccabee of Hanukkah fame, and Rabbi Akiba and Shimon bar Yohai of Lag Baomer fame, and Trumpeldor and later Mordecai Anilevitch, all of them, while post-biblical, certainly worthy of being included in the Bible. And, of course, the prophets were always there, with an important street in Haifa, Rehov Haneviim, named after them. Those prophets, starting with Samuel and Elijah and culminating with Jeremiah and the Second Isaiah, were wild characters, extremely emotional and vociferous, like many of us, Haifaites. I could relate to highly emotional and vociferous people. They remind me of a poem by Dylan Thomas,

> *Do not go gently into that good night,*
> *Rage, rage against the dying of the light.*

Those prophets were the most splendid human beings that ever walked the face of the earth. They were uninhibited, they feared no one, and they always spoke the truth, regardless of consequences. They had absolutely no respect for human authority. They usually had no power, no money, no position. They were social misfits and outcasts. They despised civilization and its discontents. They loved their people so much they spent most of their time yelling at them. They wanted them to be models of righteousness, and could not tolerate moral failings. So naturally they kept getting into trouble, but it never stopped them from getting into more trouble. There was no future in what they were doing. No job security, no retirement benefits, no social recognition. But it didn't seem to matter. They kept on prophesying.

In all my studies of religions and philosophies and social science and literature during my youth and adulthood, and in all my wanderings across the face of the earth, I have never met their equal. Humankind has had other great teachers since, Jesus and Buddha and Confucius and Muhammad and others. Those teachers have taught love and compassion and tolerance and other noble feelings. But those biblical troublemakers taught something far surpassing all noble feelings, namely, justice. Without justice, love and compassion are worthless, since all those feelings are the feelings of imperfect beings who often start out right and end up wrong. Justice, however, is transcendent and objective. It does not depend on human will. It posits that all people are equal, and deserve equal treatment. It rejects value judgments, attitudes, likes and dislikes. Pure justice does not discriminate, does not use different yardsticks for different cases. The king and the pauper are equal before it. All are treated as children of God.

All of this I was taught in 1948, and none of this has ever been surpassed or supplanted. "Behold, I have given you a good doctrine, do not forsake my Torah."

The Torah, the teaching, the sacred words of the Bible, particularly of the prophets, as interpreted in many volumes of Talmud and commentaries and Responsa, has been a light unto my feet and has guided me all my life. I have not been the most observant of Jews, and given my Haifa origins it should come as no surprise. But even as a child of eight and nine I grasped the uniqueness, the differentness of this book. As a true bookworm, I worshipped all good books, but there were two different kinds of worship. The Bible was a message from elsewhere; the other books were a message from people like myself.

45.

There was also a great sense of mystery in 1949. We were standing between worlds, disappearing worlds and new worlds. There was the disappearing world of the British Empire, a very romantic world which was coming to an end. We were part of it, and we felt very attached to it, even though we pursued our own independence. The British in many ways were our model, and despite the many conflicts of interest, we in Haifa in 1948 had great respect for the British, and did not consider them our enemy.

Then there was the world that had just disappeared in Europe, our grandparents' world of Eastern Europe, gone forever. This was so great an event we could scarcely grasp it, "we" meaning both young and adult. Even today, 50 years later, we have not yet fully grasped it. Perhaps future generations will.

And there was the disappearing world of Jews and Arabs living in Haifa side by side, mostly in peace and harmony. We certainly had our conflicts here too, but on balance it was a peaceful coexistence, and when it ended in April 1948 something very fundamental in our lives was lost forever, and we did not feel the better or the wiser for it.

And we were entering a brand new world, a world of our own making, a world of a totally new state where we had to invent everything from scratch. It was somewhat frightening, and confusing, and frustrating. But it was something we had to do.

In a word, we jumped into the unknown. And ever since then Israel has been a country which has not been afraid to jump into the unknown, even if it meant rescuing hostages in the heart of Africa or creating a new kind of fruit or signing a peace agreement with the PLO. For me, a product of Israel, jumping into the unknown has been a way of life. I have lived on different continents, learned different languages, started different careers. Even now, when most people dream about retirement, I continue to jump into the unknown.

46.

After the War of Liberation we had some harsh winters. Nature did not smile upon us, and did not make it any easier to get started. We had floods, and in early 1950 we even had snow in Haifa, for the first and only time anyone can remember. In those years hardly anyone had heating in their homes, and I recall going to bed wearing longjohns which my father had bought from U.S. Army surplus, and using all the blankets I could lay my hands on, and still shivering at night.

One day my third grade teacher, Ephratya, who lived down the street from us, told the class that many new immigrants in the Haifa area were suffering greatly from the floods. Unlike us, who were living in comfortable apartments and were protected from the elements, our newly arrived brothers and sisters who came from all the corners of the earth were living in makeshift wooden huts and army tents in new immigrant camps, known as *ma'abarot*, or transition camps. They could barely escape the torrential rains, which penetrated their living quarters, turned the walks between their homes into deep mud, and caused many of them to come down with the flu and even worse.

"We must help those poor souls," Ephratya told the class in a resolute voice. "We brought them here, and now we are responsible for their health and wellbeing."

"But what can we do?" Nurit Bester asked. Nurit was a good soul. When we boys tortured stray cats in the school yard, she would always reprimand us.

"You, children, can ask your parents to invite a child your age from one of those camps to spend the winter at your home. He or she will be like your adopted brother or sister, and besides saving them from this harsh winter, you will help them become more acclimated in their new homeland."

All the children thought it was a wonderful idea. We were

184

all going to convince our parents to invite a child from Yemen, or Morocco, or Romania to spend the winter at our home. It was the least we could do.

When I came home from school I told my mother what the teacher had told us. My mother listened with interest, and I could see the wheels turning in her head.

"Well," she finally said, "the teacher is right. It's the least we can do. "But it does raise many questions. First of all, you complain about having to share your room with your little sister. Are you willing to share it with another person?"

I told her I was willing to do it.

"And what about food? You know we are living under austerity, and can't get enough food for ourselves, let alone for another person. Are you willing to share your food?"

I told her I was.

"Well, then, are you sure your friends are also going to do it?"

"They all said they would."

"They did. But of course they will have to convince their parents, won't they?"

"Yes, of course."

"Well, we'll talk to your father, and if he agrees then we'll go ahead and do it."

I nodded in agreement.

The next day I told my teacher my parents had agreed to have a boy from the *ma'abarah* near Bat Galim stay with us for the winter. Much to my surprise, only one other person in my class had permission from his parents to do the same. And so, the only ones that day who signed up for the program were that person and I, and the teacher. The rest of my classmates had not gotten permission from their parents to host a child from the

185

ma'abarot.

My teacher made another attempt to convince the rest of the parents, but no one came through. It was an early lesson for me. Even in the most idealistic of times, most people find reasons not to do certain things which seem so obvious and necessary. True, those were difficult times, and people had little to share. But the fact remains, more people could have done what my parents, my teacher, and that other classmate of mine did, but they didn't.

I still remember that dark haired boy with the eager dark eyes and the beautiful white teeth who came to spend the winter with us. He was from Turkey, and although I no longer remember his name, I recall how grateful he was, and how well behaved, and how proud I was of my parents for doing what they did.

How did my friends and their parents feel about those new immigrants? To begin with, there was quite a cultural gap between those new arrivals and the old-timers, the *vatikim*. It was not only that the old-timers had been here longer. When my parents arrived in 1931, there were already more than a quarter million Jews in the Land of Israel who had arrived ten, twenty or more years before them. But my parents and their contemporaries were not much different from the earlier immigrants. They were all pioneers. They had all come here because of their Zionist convictions. They all had a common ideological bond, albeit they were split into different political parties, as Jews always are. With these new immigrants, however, who arrived after the birth of the state, it was altogether different. They were either Holocaust survivors, or they were Jews who had to leave hostile countries, where life had become too difficult and unsafe. Some of them, like the Yemenite Jews, were very pious, and always

186

dreamed of living in the Land of Israel. And indeed they were among those who became acclimated the fastest, and felt a deep sense of loyalty to the new state. Others had been quite assimilated, and had to relearn the meaning of a Jewish society. Others came from countries such as Egypt or Iraq, where a strong Zionist movement did not exist, and did not at first grasp the Zionist idea. And so, to begin with, there was a vast ideological gap at the time between old-timers and new arrivals.

And then there was also a cultural gap. We Israelis had patterned our lives after the West, using in many ways our British occupiers as a model. Our school system, hospital system, legal system, military system, were all patterned after the British and Western culture in general. Not so most of the new immigrants who arrived in 1948, 49 and 50. The great majority of them had come from Arab countries, and in many ways, although they prayed in Hebrew and studied the Torah and the Oral Law just like European Jews, they were nonetheless culturally more similar to the Arabs than to us. Quite a few of them came from very remote corners of the Arab world, such as Afghanistan or from the Atlas Mountains and the Sahara desert in North Africa, where they had lived among Afghan or Berber tribes, respectively. Most of those "exotic" Jews had never sat at a table to eat, and had never used a fork and a knife. Their first encounter with the new Israeli culture must have been quite a shock to them, and I am sure it was a hard painful experience for them to become acclimated in their new homeland.

I'll never forget, as a child, riding in my father's truck near the *ma'abarah* in Atlit, south of Haifa, one Saturday afternoon, and seeing a group of them standing near the camp's fence wearing their colorful pajamas. It was a very strange sight, and when I asked my father for the meaning of it, he was not quite sure what it was all about. Later on we found out that of all the clothes they were issued when they first arrived in Israel, the pajamas were the closest to the clothes they used to wear back home in North Africa or Asia, and in honor of the Sabbath they had put on their pajamas, which they felt were their best clothes...

The two major ethnic groups who came to Haifa in those early days were Moroccan and Romanian Jews. It appears that my parents and my friends' parents were not too comfortable with either group. They seemed to be afraid of the Moroccans, since they were quick-tempered and on occasion were known to pull out a knife and settle an argument by slashing their adversary. This won them the nickname "Moroccan Knife." Needless to say, many of them were mild mannered and peace loving. But the few who were not seemed to give a bad name to all the rest. As for the Romanians, who were in effect European Jews like most of the old-timers, they were generally not trusted by the latter, who dubbed them *Romeinische ganoff,* or "Romanian thief." Here again the few Romanian Jews who were dishonest gave a bad name to all the rest. Looking back, where the truth really seems to reside is in the fact that both of those ethnic groups, the Moroccans and the Romanians, were not the more educated and affluent elements of either population, but rather the ones who were forced to immigrate to the new land. To get ahead in the new and harsh reality they could not always play by the rules, and that caused hard feelings against them. In time much of this would change, but in those days everything seemed to exist in sharp contrasts of black and white, with very few grays.

47

After the war was won, there was a much greater war to win. Within a couple of years, the population of the new state would double and triple. Those who kept arriving from some one hundred different countries, had little more than the shirts on their backs. Here we were, some half a million Israeli Jews, having to house, feed, educate, provide job training, medical care and social services to some one million men, women and children, most of whom did not speak our language, and many of whom had been traumatized either by Nazi tyranny and brutality, or by dire conditions and even persecution in several Arab and Asian countries.

This new war would last for several years, and, in effect, is still being waged, especially now, in the closing years of the century, with the arrival of hundreds of thousands of Russian Jews. But there is a profound difference between the way things are now, and the way they were in 1949, 1950, and for several years thereafter. Anyone who grew up in those years will never forget the dreaded word, which dominated everyone's life, namely, *tzenah*. It was the Hebrew term for economic austerity. It meant not having enough food to eat. It meant that eating a chocolate bar was a sin. It means that eating chicken was a special occasion, and eating a steak was only a dream.

Having lived through the *tzenah*, one is grateful for every day in one's life when there is no need to worry where the next meal will come from, and whether there will be enough nourishing food to eat. Jewish culture always seemed to be keenly concerned with having enough food to eat. We who lived through the birth of the state can well understand why.

This was one chapter in my life I am not too eager to remember. Thank goodness it only lasted a few years, and did not claim too many casualties, as the 48 war did. But no retelling of the birth of the state is complete without at least a few words about the *tzenah*.

First, we had the king of *tzenah*, the economic czar, Dr. Dov Joseph. He was the most unpopular person in Israel during my childhood. In retrospect, he deserves a great deal of credit for enabling us to pull through those lean years and become a viable state. To this day, you don't hear people speak fondly of him, or, for that matter, mention him at all. Unlike our political and military heroes, men like Moshe Dayan and Ben-Gurion and several others, Dov Joseph was not a romantic figure who captured people's imagination. But perhaps in time the critical role he played in enabling Israel to survive its incredibly difficult birth will be recognized.

Dr. Joseph, a Canadian Jew with dark bushy beetle eyebrows, black thick-framed glasses, and a somber, worried expression on his long face, befitting his office, told us to "tighten our belts," and kept issuing his economic decrees from his headquarters in Jerusalem. Each person was given ration cards, which we used when we went to buy food. Nearly everything was rationed. So many eggs and so much butter per week. So much for a child and so much for an adult, and a little more for a pregnant woman, or for the sick and the infirm.

Quite naturally, alongside the rationing people invented a black market, which was conducted clandestinely, from the trunk of a car, in a dark alley, or any other discreet place. New immigrants, who had not been able to find a job, became the black marketeers. Among them, the most effective ones were Holocaust survivors, who were forced to learn the art of black marketeering during and right after the war in Europe. It was not a glorious chapter during those early days of the state, but people

191

were hungry, and a child craved a chocolate bar once in a while, and a hard working man needed some meat from time to time.

Our newly formed government looked for many ways to overcome the food scarcity, and the lack of adequate nourishment. Invariably, those attempts were not well received, and caused much resistance, especially among the children, who were not easy to fool with all sorts of food substitutes. At one point our government imported large quantities of fillet of sole from Norway (in Hebrew we called it *fileh*), and told us the fish was just as nourishing as meat or chicken. After eating *fileh* every day for two weeks, few children in Israel wanted to touch that fish, and the word *fileh* became synonymous with *tzenah*. On another occasion, large quantities of peanut butter were imported from the United States, as a substitute for real butter. Unlike American children, we had never heard of peanut butter, and as far as we were concerned it was a fake butter, another plot against us, depriving us of the real thing. Finally, our nutrition experts began to push a vegetable which grew in abundance in Israel, namely, eggplant. We were told that eggplants had as much nutritious value as meat, and should be eaten frequently. Our mother began to prepare eggplant in many different ways, and before long it became the most unpopular vegetable in Israel. For years I wouldn't eat eggplant, and only after those days were long behind us did I realize that eggplant is not so bad after all.

Another way to deal with the austerity was to receive care packages from relatives in Europe and the United States. There were special stores that handled this sort of gift. We would receive a check from our relatives abroad which we converted for something known as "scrip." We took it to that special store where we were able to exchange the scrip for such delicacies as a can of ground coffee, a salami, chocolate, and so on. Looking

192

back, I find it hard to believe we, proud Israelis, who had just won our independence, had to resort to such handouts. But again, when people are hungry they don't ask too many questions.

Somehow we survived the *tzenah*. I suppose in some ways it made us more resourceful, more sturdy, and more appreciative of the good things in life. No doubt, it played a part in accelerating the development of an agriculture and a food industry which are among the best in the world.

48.

Quite frankly, we did not have too much time in 1949 or 1950 to think about the Palestinian Arabs with whom we once lived side by side, and most of whom now lived in appalling refugee camps. We had our own camps throughout the country populated with what in effect were many thousands of displaced people, and we had to take care of them with the incredibly limited means at our disposal. We had neither the means nor the opportunity to do anything about them, and, as has been well known for years, their own Arab brothers and sisters in the neighboring countries, with all their great oil wealth, did very little to alleviate their misery. Looking back, all I can say is, "There, but for the grace of God, go I." The Arab boys I used to play with in the old neighborhood in Haifa ended up in refugee camps in Lebanon or Gaza. It could have been me. As a Jew, I am taught not to rejoice when my enemy falls, and I don't. We are all children of God, and none of us is better than anyone else. As I go back in time to my childhood years and to the birth of the state, I feel the pain they must have felt when they left Haifa. When my family and I sat at the Passover table the week after the Battle of Haifa, they were tossed at sea on boats that took them to Lebanon or to Gaza, where they would become refugees, and where for years they would dream of the breathtaking beauty of their hometown, Haifa, and, as a result, they would all become bitter, and some of them would become active in the PLO.

As a Palestinian Jew, I wish things had turned out differently with the Palestinian Arabs. The years have not taught me to hate them, in spite of all the terrorist acts of the last half century. In many ways, the Arab world is a very conflicted world, with many human problems that wait to be resolved. But in the final analysis we Jews and our Arab neighbors share a common fate. We belong to the same part of the world, and we have no choice but to learn how to live in peace side by side. Any other approach to our conflict is sheer lunacy. By seeking to destroy us, they have caused enormous damage to themselves, and by seeking to destroy them, we court our own doom. Every Israeli does not have to love every Arab, or vice versa. Nor, for that matter, does every Israeli love every other Israeli, or every Arab every other Arab. But the rule of "live and let live" is the only rule we can live by, and the sooner we learn it the better.

195

49.

They came from all over the world. Everyone came to Israel in those days. My cousins Genia and Ellen and Bernard Mintz from France, Uncle José from Uruguay, cousin Moteleh the Hasid from New York, cousin Moteleh Abrabanel from Auschwitz, and others whom I must have forgotten. They all had amazing, incredible stories to tell (we've already heard the story of Moteleh Abrabanel). They were all looking to start a new life. Israel seemed the natural place for them to try out. But hardly any of them stayed. They all had better options. Unlike the thousands of refugees from Eastern and Central Europe and from the Arab world, they had a place to go back to. Paris, Montevideo, New York, all those places appeared very attractive when one had to struggle to make ends meet in post-Liberation War Israel. Many of them stayed with us for a while, sleeping on cots on the big balcony, sharing our rationed food. We did whatever we could to help them adjust to the Promised Land. But the temptation to go back was too great, and we too were infected by it.

They were colorful characters, all of them, and I was fascinated by their stories. First there was Jean Brauman from Paris, Genia's fiance. He was a dashing young Air Force officer, incredibly strong, with a small French mustache, mischievous eyes, and a constant smile. As a teenager during the Nazi occupation in France he joined the French underground, or the *Resistance*. He lived in constant danger, but had the satisfaction of spending the war years inflicting losses and casualties on those who sent his relatives to the death camps. When the war ended he felt aliented from his native France, since most Frenchmen -- notwithstanding their amnesia and revisionism after the war -- did not support the Resistance and even betrayed it. He did not see any future for himself as a Jew in France, and decided to join the new Israeli army. He saw some action during the end of our war, and after the war became Golda Meir's personal chauffeur. My cousin, Genia, a beautiful blond whom he met in Paris after the war, followed him to Israel. My parents arranged their wedding during the height of the war. It was a very small wedding, and we had to get a special permit to obtain the igredients for baking a wedding cake, an unheard of luxury during that time. We went to a small restaurant on Jerusalem Street to celebrate the wedding, and the most beautiful part of it was Genia's wedding gown. It was truly resplendent, and the young blond, blue eyed Genia looked in it like a young Jane Fonda. The picture of the bride and groom was shown in the photographer's window on Herzl Street (the same one who had displayed the picture of my sister Dahlia and myself) for a very long time. They might as well have won the prize for the most attractive couple to be married during the War of Liberation.

After the war they were given a beautiful vacant Arab stone villa in Dir Abu Tur in Jerusalem, which commanded some of the best views of the city. As far as young couples starting out in Israel go, they were off to a pretty good start. But Genia missed Paris. She missed the glamour of *La Ville Lumière*. And so, after their first son, Ronnie, was born, they went back. Ronnie became a famous humanitarian physician, president of the famous European organizaton Doctors without Frontiers. He could have made a major contribution to Israeli medicine. For the rest of his life, his father, Jean, would dream of resettling in Israel, but it appears it was not meant to be.

Another French cousin who was very anxious to settle in Israel in those days was Bernard Mintz, from Lyon, France. Bernard was raised by a Catholic family during World War Two, since his mother, Aunt Rivka, had to hide from the Nazi occupiers in the South of France, and could not well remain mobile with a little boy in tow. So she gave him to some nice Roman Catholic French neighbors, where he was raised as a Catholic boy. There were many such incidents in France. Those Jewish parents lucky to remain alive came back to reclaim their child. Many never came back, and the children were lost to Judaism. One such child was Cardinal Lustinger, the head of the Catholic Church in Paris, purported to be a very good friend of the Jews and Israel.

After the war Bernard completed France's most prestigious school of engineering with distinction. He was a mathematical genius. As a civil engineer, he could look at a bridge or a building and tell you within seconds exactly how much iron and concrete went into the construction of that particular structure. He could have been of enormous use to the Ministry of Housing and Construction of the new government of Israel, except for one thing. As a young man of about thirty, he was expected to serve in the new Israeli army. Bernard had an aversion to weapons and soldiering, and refused to be drafted. If Israel has had some very rigid rules over the years, the rule of military service is perhaps the most rigid. So no ingenious solution was found for Bernard's problem, and he went back to France, where he became one of the top civil engineers for the French government, and was sent to Africa to work on some very large construction projects. Bernard became a prominent member of the Jewish community of Lyon, and, I was told, is quite wealthy. As a child I used to play chess with him, and he always beat me. But I liked him for his honesty and integrity, and I am sorry he did not stay in Israel, where he could have made a major contribution to the building of the new state.

Uncle José came to visit from South America after the state was born. He was my mother's younger brother. When he was seventeen he had to join the Polish army. He had no desire to become a Polish soldier, and neither did his parents. He took a trip to Uruguay and stayed there for over thirty years, where he married my aunt Fanny, who also happens to be my father's cousin, and raised a family. In the sixties he finally moved to Israel, and so did his two daughters, who gave rise to families in Jerusalem. Uncle José was part of a large number of East European Jews who might have liked to go to Israel long before, but were not able to. They spent a good part of their lives in South America, in countries like Argentina, Uruguay, or Chile. But eventually they came, and most of them stayed. South America, with all its socio-economic problems, did not lure them back, as Paris did to my Parisian cousin, Genia. Few ever went back to South America.

My cousin Moteleh first came to Israel in 1949 for a short visit. I was ten. He was twelve. He came with his father, who was married to a cousin of my mother's. His father was a Belz Hasid. My mother's father was also a Belz Hasid. So were my two uncles, whom I had never met. My mother hated the Belze rebbe, the leader of the Belz Hasidim. He had tried to talk her father out of letting her go to the land of Israel. She blamed him for the fact that her brothers, who were closet Zionists, remained in Europe and perished in the Holocaust. The Holocaust was a watershed in Hasidic history. More than a million Hasidim perished in the Holocaust. Many surivors ceased to be Hasidim after the Great Catasrophe, while others clung to the old movement with greater tenacity than before. Moteleh's father was one of them. During the Holocaust he hid with his family in

199

Belgium, where they learned the trade of diamond cutting, which they took with them to New York after the war. Little Moteleh studied in a Catholic school, and had no idea he was a Hasid. Soon after the war, when he was eight, his father took him to a barber to shave his head, and let his sidelocks grow, according to the Hasidic custom. Moteleh was deeply affected by this experience, and he knew then and there he had to leave that world of religious extremism.

Hasidism has been deeply rooted in my soul. Deep inside of me I am a Hasid. But at the same time I am my mother's son, and I could never assume the Hasidic way of life. Moteleh, my cousin, and my childhood intimate friend, rebelled against Hasidism. He started reading books about Zionism in his home in Brooklyn against his father's orders. He read Herzl and Ahad Haam and Hess, and he decided to settle in Israel, which he later did. His decision to leave the Hasidic community was not an easy one. It meant breaking with his family and friends, and starting a new, unknown life. With him, it was never a clean break, but rather a torturous, circuitous road, that took him into the Israeli Army, than into the U.S. Army, then back to Israel, where he married a lovely young woman from Iraq, and then back to the States. I finally lost track of him, but recently I rediscovered him by sheer accident. He now holds a prestigious position at Yad Vashem in Jerusalem. During my childhood in Israel he was one of the most influential friends I had, who helped shape my own personal identity.

50.

I started reading newspapers at a very young age. My father used to bring home a newspaper called *Haaretz*, The Land, and as soon as I was able to read I would retrieve the paper after my parents discarded it and go slowly through its lines and columns. Most of what I read I did not understand. Who was that "Winston Churchill" they kept writing about? Who was the "High Commissioner?" What did the word "inflation" mean? Not recognizing a name or understanding a word did not deter me from reading on. I was fascinated by the mystery of those names adults kept mentioning, and I was intrigued by long words with foreign sounds. When I started learning English in third grade I tried to read a paper called *Palestine Post*, which would soon change its name to *Jerusalem Post*. Actually, I recall working on my English in my young teens by reading American magazines such as *Life, Look, Time*, and the *Saturday Evening Post*. I would make long lists of words, look them up in the dictionary, and try to memorize them. At thirteen I signed up for a French class in some evening school and started reading *Paris Match,* and at age fourteen, when I began high school, I was introduced to the study of Arabic, and read a newspaper called *Al Yaum* (The Day).

In 1948 a new afternoon daily made its appearance in the newly born state. It was called *Maariv*. It saw the light of day during the War of Independence, and had to overcome a great deal of adversity. I recall how the entire paper consisted of a single sheet, printed on both sides. In that limited space the paper tried to cover national and international news, provide editorials, human interest stories, photographs, humor, and even some display ads and classified notices. The young crew that started that paper made up in talent for what it lacked materially, and in time *Maariv* would become for many years the most widely read paper in Israel, with many supplements and a weekend edition of well over a hundred pages.

The founder and editor in chief of *Maariv* was Dr. Azriel Carlbach. He soon started to publish a weekly article on the weekends in which he offered his observations on life in the new state. Not to read a Carlbach article meant not to be truly informed of what was going on in the new state. One of the routine activities every Saturday in Israel in the early years was a discussion of Carlbach's latest article. I would probably not be exaggerating if I said that those articles helped shape our national character. Recently, while going through some of Carlbach's early articles, dating back to 1948, I found an article titled "Haifa, the New York of Asia." It was published on August 31, 1948, during the ceasefire, and did not attract much attention. First, because there was a war going on, and we were fighting for our survival. Second, because it was a visionary article which dared predict the future, an activity which has been discouraged among Jews for over two thousand years, since the time of the prophets. Rereading it now, nearly fifty years later, one cannot help but marvel at Carlbach's ability to predict the future.

The article begins with the familiar joke which attempts to explain why, of all places, Moses brought the Israelites to this arid strip of land between the desert and the sea, a land that has seen so much strife and turmoil throughout the centuries. Why couldn't the great prophet Moses have picked a more lush and peaceful country, at some less eventful corner of the world? Well, as the Bible tells us, Moses was a stutterer. When the Almighy asked Moses to pick a country, Moses had his sights on Canada. He started saying, "Ca, ca, ca," unable to finish articulating the next two syllables. The Almighy grew impatient and blurted out, "Okay, I'll give you the land of Canaan." Once the divine word was spoken, it became impossible to change it.

By retelling this joke, the eminent journalist was taking to task the nay-sayers of the Yishuv, whose number was never small, those who chose to take a pessimistic view of the future prospects of the infant state. He goes on to make his point that despite all the difficulties of the present moment, a great future lies ahead for the new state. He predicts that once this highly strategic point of the globe becomes an independent Jewish state, the Jewish genius would not only make the desert bloom, but would in effect turn this tiny land into a world center of trade, science and technology.

Carlbach draws an interesting comparison between the American and the Israeli experience of overthrowing British rule and building a great nation. He must have visited New York in November 1947, when he covered the historical UN vote at Lake Success, Long Island. Seeing the skyscrapers in Manhattan made him think not of Tel Aviv or Jerusalem, but rather of Haifa. He tells us he was standing at the southern tip of Manhattan, near the harbor, which probably made him think of Haifa harbor. Then he looked north at Fifth Avenue, and the thought occurred to him that some day Haifa too would have high rise buildings and would become a world center of trade and many other activities like New York City (hence the title of this article - Haifa, the New York of Asia).

I vividly recall what Haifa looked like in 1948. The tallest buildings we had had four stories, maybe five. The slopes of Mount Carmel were sprinkled with clusters of mostly one or two story white houses. A small, dormant Mediterranean town. But Carlbach was able to see the Haifa of 1998, half a century later. A city with large buildings stretching deep into the hills and valleys of the Carmel in the east, along the coast in the south, and almost as far as Acre in the north. A city which boasts some of Israel's best known high tech industries, indeed, a world metropolis.

Exactly fifty years before Carlbach wrote this article, Dr. Herzl wrote, "If not in five, then in fifty years there will be a Jewish state." He was right. Today, fifty years later, we can see Carlbach's was also right. And now, since every fifty years some Jew makes a prediction, I will make my own: Fifty years hence, around the middle of the twenty-first century, if not sooner, the United Nations will reside in Jerusalem, rather than New York, and the state of Israel will play a special role between the West and the East, a role of peacemaking and reconciliation.

51.

One of the most fascinating experiences of my childhood was a class trip to Nazareth, to the holy places of Christianity. Nazareth is less than an hour by car from Haifa. In this town the most famous Jew in the world grew up. Since my childhood I was always intrigued and inspired by the life and teachings of Jesus of Nazareth.

Which is quite strange, since my Israeli contemporaries seemed to have little interest in this subject. We all knew that in the name of the gentle teacher from the Galilee we Jews were persecuted for two thousand years. It was a subject better left alone, for we were now becoming a nation like all other nations, with a strong Western orientation, and we had to find new ways to get along with the Christian world. As for me, at age ten I read the New Testament in Hebrew translation (a copy of the New Testament was left in our house by some missionaries, and I kept it), and was quite taken with the stories of the Gospels. While the idea of a person, especially a fellow-Jew, becoming divine did not quite work for me, I had no doubt here that was a very special person, unlike anyone else I had ever known, read or studied about, even unlike the characters in the Hebrew Bible, which Christians refer to as the Old Testament. When our fifth grade teacher announced a class trip to Nazareth, I was probably the most eager and willing person in the class. I felt I was about to learn one of the most important lessons my native land had to offer, namely, the source of a belief that has practically swept the entire human race.

I was not disappointed. Nazareth was an Arab city, populated by Arab Christians. But there was no mistaking the fact that what had taken place in this modest city in the Lower Galilee had affected the lives of more people around the world

205

than anything else before or after. This town was once home to a carpenter named Joseph, whose shop is still shown in the basement of one of the churches. He had a son name Yeshu, or Joshua. One of the toughest problems I had was understanding the divine birth, which was dramatized at a beautiful church built by the Vatican in Nazareth, called the Church of the Annunciation. To me it made perfect sense that a boy who was born in Nazareth, rather than Bethlehem, to a carpenter and his wife, became a wondrous teacher of humankind. The landscape of the Galilee around Nazareth, especially Mount Beatitudes, where Jesus gave the Sermon on the Mount, was a perfect setting for the teachings of the Gospels. The famous fables taking place in villages around Nazareth, such as Kannah, or at the Sea of Galilee, fit in perfectly with the landscape and the mood of the place, and seemed to have little to do with the escape to Egypt, or the Magi Kings in Bethlehem, or any of the other stories which may have very well been apocryphal.

The class trip to Nazareth was one of the highlights of my childhood. My interest in Christianity continued to grow since that day. To me, even as a child, Jesus was a good Jew, a spiritual disciple of Hillel, the great and gentle rabbi of the century preceding his. Much of his teachings was altered by later generations, and little was observed by those who worshiped him. I am always reminded of the chapter in the book *The Brothers Karamazov,* titled "The Great Inquisitor," which argues that if Jesus came back to earth, his followers would crucify him all over again. To me, Jesus was crucified at least six million times during World War Two, when so many or more of his brothers and sisters were done unto death by so-called Christians. To me, a native of northern Israel, a fellow-countryman of Jesus, he will always remain one of the great teachers of humanity, whose lessons are worth heeding, not only by those who call themselves Christians, but by everyone.

52.

What was the place you liked the most when you were a kid? Which place did you want to go back to over and over again, and never got tired of?

For me and my friends in Haifa at the time following the birth of the state that place was the communal swimming pool at Bat Galim.

Bat Galim is a lovely little seaside suburb of Haifa on the Mediterranean shore, south of Haifa Harbor. The pool at Bat Galim, an Olympic size pool where Maccabiah games were held in those days, with an Olympic diving tower and large bleachers, with a small beach next to it, and food concessions and games predating today's video games, was our idea of what paradise was like. During the summer vacation, which we called the Great Vacation, we would go there practically every day. You were always sure to meet your friends there. The water in the pool was sea water, pumped in from the sea and drained back into the sea. Over the years I have known bigger and better pools, but none has ever surpassed the Bat Galim pool. It was not just the pool, but everything around it. The sea, the sky, the beach next to it, the hot corn on the cob, the ice cold watermelon and juicy prickly pears, the spicy falafel, the Artik and Kartiv ice cream bars and fruit flavored ice bars, the games, everything. It was as if the Master of the Universe has ordained it, as if it were part of creation itself, along with Adam and Eve and the Garden of Eden. Life to us was inconceivable without that pool. If there was a reason for our coming into this world, it was probably the pool at Bat Galim.

I spent my entire childhood and teens at that pool. I fell in love and out of love with girls my age at this pool more times than I can remember. When I left Haifa in my late teens I never saw the pool again. But it lived in my memory and in my dreams all these years. Whenever I thought happy thoughts, somehow they were always associated with that pool. Thoughts of love, peace of mind, success, somehow were all connected to that pool, as though it were some sacred shrine where one always brought one's thanks offerings. Finally, last year, when I went back to Haifa to visit the places described in this book, I decided to revisit the Bat Galim pool.

I had no difficulty finding the way to Bat Galim, driving directly from the German Colony. I arrived at the grounds of the pool and parked my car off the road above the small beach next to the pool. The pool was hidden from view by a high cement wall. I walked down to the beach. The old wharf was still there, as in the old days. I turned left and walked along the beach towards the pool. When I reached the gate to the pool I couldn't believe my eyes. The pool was no longer there. There was a large gaping hole in the ground and huge slabs of cement and twisted iron rods scattered about. The Bat Galim pool, the place of my dreams, was gone.

When I drove back to the city I suddenly burst into tears. I cried like a child, uncontrollably. I must have felt the way Adam felt when he was banished from the Garden of Eden. Suddenly, I became aware of my mortality. I had hoped the pool of my dreams would be there forever. But forever only seems to exist in our minds, not in real life. But then, who knows, perhaps some day someone will rebuild the pool at Bat Galim.

53

As a close second to the pool came the movies. Abbott and Costello. Gary Cooper. Tyrone Power. Robert Taylor. Charlie Chaplin. Ingrid Bergman. Silvana Mangano. The Russian propaganda movies. Maurice Schwartz. Paul Muni. Humphrey Bogart. Linda Darnell. Virginia Mayo. World War Two movies. And, of course, the Wild West.

We absolutely loved and adored the movies. We children usually went to the three-thirty matinee. During the afternoon show the movie theater belonged to us. We would start arriving at two-thirty, and by three-thirty the place was pandemonium. The noise level in the theater was at least that of a hard rock band, if not louder. Everyone was shouting above everyone else's voice. Every few seconds a fight broke out. Rival groups from different youth organizations or schools would start taunting each other, itching for a fight. Someone would yell out,

"All the girls at Bialik School put out."

"All the boys at Hugim School are castrated," the Bialik group would yell back.

"Would you like to see my balls?" the he-man of the Hugim School said, standing up and unbuckling his belt.

The Bialik girls started screaming, more gleeful than frightened, I suspect.

The belt was now open, and the fly was next. In those days we did not have zipper flies, but rather buttons.

By now there are two Bialik boys eyeballing the he-man. He shoves them aside. They recover their balance and swing at him. He grabs both their heads and bang them together. His name is Gideon. He is a distant cousin of mine. Some day he'll become a ship captain for Zim, the Israeli merchant marine.

No one messes with Gideon. He is not the strongest kid in

the theater, but he is one hundred percent daredevil. He does not stop at anything. His head has already been stitched up on six or seven different occasions. He is the quintessential *Sabra*, or native Israeli.

Most of us are onlookers, letting others do the fighting. We come to the theater equipped with bags of salted sunflower seeds, a Middle East delicacy. We are all experts at cracking sunflower seeds in our mouths. We toss a seed into our mouth, grab it between our upper and lower molers, crack it open, easing the seed with our tongue out of the shell, and spitting the shell on the floor. By the time the movie is over, the entire floor of the theater is covered with a two-to-three-inch layer of sunflower shells. It takes about an hour for the ushers, who have to clean the theater for the evening performance, to sweep the shells off the floor.

After the theater darkens, it takes us about ten minutes to quiet down. It is a good thing we have Hebrew subtitles. If we had to listen to the dialogue, we would miss the beginning and never find out what the movie was all about. As soon as the hero kisses the heroine, everyone starts whistling, hooting, pounding the floor with his feet, and yelling *tiras ham*, or "hot corn on the cob." Someone points at the boys sitting in the front row, and says, "They want to be able to look under the women's skirts, those dummies."

Somehow we make it through the movie. The fact is, we get emotionally involved with nearly all those movies, with very few exceptions. A movie has to be incredibly boring for us not to get involved in. We look upon those movie stars as some kind of mythological beings, larger than life, capable of incredible feats and great, superhuman passions. It doesn't occur to us that some of us are capable of much greater feats than, say, Gary Cooper or

211

John Wayne. While they are posing, we are part of one of the great miracles of history, and some of us will some day do in real life what Cooper or Wayne only do on the screen. But then, they appear on the screen ten feet tall, while we are somewhere between five and six feet, for the most part.

Whenever I see a rerun of one of the movies we saw in those days, I am transported back to those warm afternoons inside the air-conditioned theater in Haifa (it was one of the few air-conditioned places in town back then, which added greatly to the thrill), and I can still see Gideon challenging everyone in the theater, and I can feel the excitement I felt back then, when the movies appeared more real than life, and we, the children of the dream, spent two hours bewitched by the greatest dream factory of all.

54.

In May 1949 we celebrated the first birthday of the infant state. That year and for the next several years the yearly celebration known as Independence Day was an incredibly joyous occasion. The joy and excitement of those early independence days have remained with me all these years. It says in the Talmud, "He who did not experience the joy of Beit Hashoevah never experience joy in his life." This statement refers to the celebration of the Feast of Tabernacles by the pilgrims who went up to Jerusalem at the time of the Temple. In a way, we were reliving those ancient days, when the Temple existed, and when Jews were free people in their own land. As a child of ten and as a young teenager, I fully experienced the joy of "a free people in our own land, the land of Zion and Jerusalem," and I thrilled at the great military parades, but there was something else which was even more thrilling. It was the fact that we children were allowed to stay up all night, celebrating, singing, dancing, and beginning to discover all those boy-girl mysteries. For one whole night the entire city of Haifa became one big party, one big celebration, and we, the young, were free to dance in the streets, go around party-hopping, hitchhike up and down the mountain, or celebrate with our different youth movements, in my case the Tzofim, or Scouts.

Over the years, the excitement of *Yom Ha'atzmaut* diminished. But in the early days it was magic. And it was felt by all, young and adult alike. The poet Shin Shalom wrote a song about it, which we sang on that occasion:

> *Friends, let us say the blessing "Who has kept us alive,"*
> *Let us lift a cup to the life of the state,*
> *For happy are we to have reached this moment,*

For we willed it, and it is no dream.

55.

The dominent figure in Israel in 1949 was old man Ben-Gurion, whose picture was in the papers almost every day. I mean no disrespect, but Ben-Gurion, as I knew him in those days, was not a very likable person. In later life I had the honor and privilege of getting to know his arch political opponent, Menachem Begin. If I had to choose between the two as a personal friend, I would not hesitate for a moment and choose Begin. But looking back, Ben-Gurion, basically a hard, unfeeling person, had qualities which were necessary for establishing the new state. Begin, on the other hand, notwithstanding his terrorist image, was kind, caring, and emotional, qualities which would endear a person as a friend, but will not always work well in times of crisis.

Who am I to even dare to discuss these great men? Their greatness grows as the years go by, and will continue to grow. They are the founding fathers of the Third Commonwealth, and enough nonsese has already been written about both of them. Surely there is no need for me to add more.

I only wish to do some reminiscing about that stocky superenergetic little man with the shiny red balding head and the crown of wavy white hair, as I knew him when the state started in the late forties and early fifties.

How did I feel about him in those days, as a child? I started out by saying he was not a very likable person, which demands an explanation. What do I base myself on? Both on my personal experience and on what many people have told me and have written about him. I remember one time my father took me to hear Ben-Gurion speak at the Armon Theater in Haifa. We sat on the balcony. There was a long table on the stage, occupied by Ben-Gurion's Labor Party's leaders and activists. He stood in the middle behind the table and gave his usual fiery speech. All of a sudden a man stood up in the audience and shouted:

"There are four hundred men out of work in Haifa!"

Ben-Gurion stopped talking. There was a moment of electrifying silence. Everyone waited to hear what the Prime Minister would say in response to that anguished call for help. I myself expected something like, "Don't worry, you will soon be back to work." Instead, Ben-Gurion's face turned red and he shouted at his heckler, "I didn't ask you!" At first, there was a stunned silence in the audience, when suddenly the men on the stage got up, facing their leader, and burst into a thunderous applause. It was a signal for the many party loyalists in the audience to follow suit, which they did, half-heartedly.

My father was not a follower of Ben-Gurion, and, in addition, he was a very sensitive person. He found the whole scene rather objectionable. I myself never forgot it. Even at the young age of ten in made a lasting impression on me.

The above incident was typical of Ben-Gurion. My fourth grade teacher, Yosef Goldstein, used to say that Ben-Gurion only loved two things -- himself and the IDF. I am not quite sure this is a fair statement. The problem with Ben-Gurion was not one of not caring, but of not knowing how to show his feelings. I am sure he cared about that unemployed worker in Haifa who heckled him during his speech. But that was a typical Ben-Gurion reaction -- harsh, unfeeling. And I have little doubt in my mind that his personality had a great influence on the Israeli national character, which suffers from a lack of sensitivity, and has a harsh edge to it. I think Ben-Gurion's personality rubbed off on one of his main disciples, Moshe Dayan, and affected him in a rather adverse way, which made Dayan altogether unfit to become the leader of the nation, as Ben-Gurion had hoped he would. A later disciple, Yitzhak Rabin, was also influenced by the Ben-Gurion syndrome, and although he had overcome much of it, he was never too pleasant a person to deal with, as I once found out for myself during his tenure as the Israeli ambassador to Washington.

It is not fair to put the full burden of the so-called "Israeli character" on the "old man." He was not the only harsh character around in my childhood. There were quite a few other Ben-Gurion-like personalities, who could have used a measure of kindness and compassion. One of them was Dr. Biram, the founder of my high school in Haifa, the Reali School, known for producing Israeli generals. He was a Prussian Jew who was more German than the Germans, and the founder of military education in Israel. Another was the future mayor of Haifa, Abba Khoushi. And the list is quite long. Ironically, most of these men were socialists, and yet their behavior was much more authoritarian than social. It was left to others, who did not preach socialism, to be more kind and social.

So Ben-Gurion was certainly not the kind fatherly figure. Rather, he was the boss, the man in charge, the one who made sure things got done. He was respected and appreciated. But was he loved? Well, he made it quite difficult for people to love him. And I have a feeling he did not want to be loved. He had an aversion for feelings, which to him must have spelled weakness. He was a single-minded man with a mission, whose mind must have been locked on that mission day and night, to the exclusion of everything else. The last time I saw him, in 1970, when he was in his eighties, he was still completely locked into his mission. "The State of Israel is not here yet," he told me and my colleagues. "We may have the beginning of a state, but we don't yet have a real, full-fledged state. This will take time."

Looking back, he was indeed the father of the state. But I

217

wish he had been kinder and gentler, or at least endowed with a sense of humor. Perhaps this was too much to ask.

56.

We all had our colors, so to speak, in those days. Some of us wore khaki shirts, some blue, and some brown. And it seemed to make a big difference which color shirt your wore. The khaki was worn by the Scouts. We were the political middle-of-the-road, more interested in scouting than politicking. Our parents belonged to either the centrist, left of center, or right of center parties. They were not political radicals. The blue shirts belonged to the extreme left, especially Hashomer Hatzair, who were somewhat Marxist, and looked down on everyone else as either bourgeois, fascist, decadent, misguided, or hypocritical. They had a proclivity for using strong language when describing ideologies that did not quite agree with their own. Many of them were quite nice people, but there was something naive about their political fundamentalism. The strongholds of the radical left were the kibbutzim around Haifa, not so much the city itself. City life seemed to make people less politically radical, while the kibbutz society was a closed world where one could indulge in all sorts of radical views, much like a monastic order or an academic community, where one does not have to worry so much about the real world. To the extreme right were the brown shirts, or light brown, namely, the Revisionist Zionists, the disciples of Jabotinsky, whose youth movement was known as Beitar, or, in the underground, the Irgun, or the Etzel. Those were rare in Haifa. In fact, there seemed to be a broad general consensus in Haifa against them, and when I grew up they were not even allowed to walk in the street in their brown shirts. Some of them were extremely brave, and from time to time would attempt to take a walk on Herzl Street in their brown uniforms. This stroll would invariably end up in a fist fight, with several "blue shirts" or even "khaki shirts" ganging up on the one brown shirt, sending him running with a bruised face and a bleeding nose.

The world has greatly changed since those days. Politics is not the matter of life and death it used to be. But the political culture of the years of the birth of the state has had a great impact on the life of Israel to this day. For many Israelis, politics has taken the place of religion. Even as different religious sects proliferated among the Jews in Eastern Europe in past centuries, Israelis are still divided into over twenty political parties, a rather large number for a small nation, and every four years new parties seem to crop up. While their grandparents and great-grand-parents in Romania or Poland used to gossip constantly about the rabbi and the members of his family, they talk constantly about their political leaders and their families. All of this began when the state was born. As soon as the British left, every party in Israel geared up for the elections to the new elected bodies of the new state, especially the Knesset, which consisted of 120 members. Every imaginable party, no matter how small, came up with a list of 120 candidates for the Knesset. In some cases, those 120 represented nearly all the people who voted for that particular party, but it didn't seem to matter. Among Jews, everyone is a leader, or at least everyone thinks he or she is.

An enormous amount of time, money and energy was spent on election day in the early years of the infant state, which was quite amazing, since the country was flat broke. To me, as a child, it all appeared like some kind of a mad carnival. We had those large billboards in the streets in those days, about fifteen feet long and eight feet tall, on which everything imaginable was advertised, from death announcements to a new movie. During election week those billboards were completely covered with election posters. Each party was assigned a letter or a combination of letters in the Hebrew alphabet. The leading labor party had the letter Aleph, and they decorated it with a sheaf of wheat twined around the massive leg of the first Hebrew letter, made to look like a hammer. Next followed all the other parties. In addition to the letters, there were slogans. The loftiest words imaginable were conjured up by each party. One party announced: "Justice, Brotherhood, Peace." The other countered: "Others Promise, We Deliver." A third one added: "They All Promise, We Do." There was no end to the self-righteousness of all those parties. If they only kept one percent of their promises, we would have long since reached a state of utopia.

The last few days before the elections reached a feverish pitch. You could see people having political debates on every street corner. Voices were raised, tempers flared up, and fistfights were common. Although paper was rationed like everything else, there seemed to be plenty of paper when it came to campaign posters, leaflets, brochures, or just small pieces of paper which simply had the letter of the party printed on them. These abounded like confetti, and seemed to be everywhere, like some sort of a strange plague. You almost got the impression that each party felt that if it did not win the world would come to an end.

On one such election week I was drafted by the General Zionist party to distribute leaflets at the poll. I was paid the impressive sum of five Israeli pounds for spending four hours in front of the poll. It was one of my first jobs ever, and I was quite thrilled to at least get something out of this entire election madness. I did my work faithfully, shoving the leaflets in people's faces. The next day I had to go to the General Zionists office on Balfour Street to collect my five pounds. As it turned out, this party did very poorly in that particular election (it had started to decline after the birth of the state), and the disbursement office never opened to pay all of us kids who did all the hard work for those fine politicians. We never collected our money, but we did come back the next night with some well chosen stones which left most of the windows at this party's headquarters shattered.

I never found politics to be the finest aspect of life in my native land.

57.

The years following the birth of the state took their toll on my parents. My father was now in his forties, and he could no longer pull off those physical feats of his youth. His work, transporting fish from Haifa to the rest of the country, did not get any easier. As the population grew, his work volume grew as well, and he made several attempts to take on a partner. But none lasted more than a few months. Some of them were young and strong, but they could not keep up with the routine of getting up in the middle of the night, driving a truck for hours, and then turning around to start another run.

Today we call this phenomenon "burnout." The years of war and hard labor in the Promised Land always produced a great deal of burnout. At least half of my schoolmates from those days no longer live in Israel, even though we were part of the privileged class and had many opportunities. Some of them were gone in their teens with their families. Others left after they finished the army, invariably to study abroad, where they found jobs and remained.

Looking back on those years, I marvel at how people like my parents were able to do all the things they did. In a sense, they had to lead a double life. They had to do all the things all people do everywhere, make a living, raise a family, get some enjoyment out of life. At the same time they had to respond to all sorts of communal and national missions, help the defense effort, help the newcomers, sacrifice in every way imaginable for the state to survive. It was no wonder they suffered burnout in the fifties, during the early years of the state. It is a miracle Israel overcame that difficult time altogether and went on to become what it is today.

58.

When 1950 started, we had an infant state, a little over a year and a half old. The war was now over. The new immigrants were freezing in their makeshift camps. We were all cursing the *tzenah* and its czar. The Arabs were preparing for the next war, and we were all becoming soldiers (an Israeli is a perpetual soldier who is on leave either part or most of the year). Those were some of the most memorable features of that year. By now we had sold our grocery store and my father was discharged from the army and went back to transporting fish for Tnuvah. My mother was now pregnant with her third child, and my parents decided to buy a larger apartment. They were building new four story apartment buildings on Arlozoroff Street, not far from the Bahai Temple, on the way to the top of Mount Carmel. My parents took the money they had gotten from the sale of the store and bought a three bedroom apartment, quite a luxury item in those days. Personally, I was delighted with this new apartment, first and foremost because for the first time in my life I was given my own room. My parents, who were quite aware and supportive of my literary interests, told me they were actually going to buy me a grownup desk, made of mahogany wood with a glass top, and wooden bookcases with glass doors. And, to top it all off, they were going to buy me a Hebrew typewriter, an item even my schoolteachers did not own. I was the happiest kid on the block.

The apartment had other advantages, which were not lost on me. First off, it was located in a beautiful mountain area, where one could go roaming, picking figs off wild figtrees, or, at times, even sneaking into the beautiful fruit gardens of the Bahai Temple and stealing some grapes or apricots or kumquats. Finally, the most remarkable feature of that apartment was a long and wide balcony that ran the length of the apartment in the back, overlooking the entire city of Haifa, the harbor, the bay, and the mountains of Lebanon in the distance. Much of our daily life took place on that balcony. We ate most of our meals out there, savoring the view. Sometimes, on hot nights, we even slept there. And on one end of the balcony we enclosed a square area with an aluminum frame and a canvas, and used it as a storage area.

Oddly enough, 1950 started in Haifa with a snow. To my knowledge, it never snowed before or after in this semi-tropical town. I recall sitting in class that afternoon, on Pevzner Street, in the center of Haifa. It was a dark, dreary afternoon, and it was unusually cold. Suddenly our teacher stopped talking to the class and went to the window.

"There is something going on outside," he said, "something you won't believe."

We all rushed to the windows. Around this time of year the almond trees began to flower in Israel, and were clad in a magnificent robes of white and pink blossoms. We looked at the rain outside and at first we thought we were looking at a shower of almond blossoms.

"Snow," the teacher finally said the magic word.

"Snow? In Haifa? impossible!"

"Well, pupils, you have the rest of the period off. You are all free to go outside and enjoy the snow."

And enjoy it we did. We were soon teaming up in the schoolyard in small groups, and we started a snowball war the like of which I have never experienced again. Those snowballs flew across the yard in every direction. You could see who the champion throwers were, and who were the slouches. Yitzhak Fuchs, Dror Avivi, and Shmuel Schmorak were the champions. The rest of us were the second string.

225

But it didn't really matter how good you were at throwing snowballs. Everyone was having the time of their lives. For two days Haifa was covered with a white virginal blanket of snow. Older Jews from Austria and Germany who still had their old skiing equipment took it out and skied down Hess and Balfour Streets. People who as children in Europe used to build snowmen, made a commendable attempt to do the same here, although the supply was not as abundant as it was in the old country. As for the rest of us, namely, the *Sabras,* or native born Israelis, we made our first acquaintance with the white marvel.

Nineteen-fifty was a year of many firsts. In fact, most things happening in the new state were a first. In our household, we had a phone installed for the first time. My mother, who was not one given to idle talk, nonetheless spent quite a bit of time on the phone talking to her friends who also had phones. It must have been something truly irresistible. The only one who did not benefit from the phone was my father. He would now receive phone calls at all hours, day and night, to come down to the harbor to pick up the fish. His life, rather than getting easier with the new truck, new apartment, and many other new things, became more difficult.

I have never met anyone who worked harder than my father. He used to go out before the crack of dawn to the harbor downtown, and have his truck loaded with fish crates. He took the fish to Tel Aviv or Jerusalem, where it was unloaded at the Tnuvah warehouse, for distribution to the fish dealers in those cities. As soon as they finished unloading, he would turn around and drive back to Haifa, a drive of two to three hours. He would then load another truckful and back he went. This often went on for a day, a night, and another day at a time. When he came

226

home at the end of a series of deliveries, his eyes were bloodshot and his brain barely functioned. He would collapse on his bed and sleep for several hours, and then go back again. It was an inhuman workload. He did make good money, better than most people in Haifa in those days, but at too high a cost to his health and well-being. My mother made constant efforts to change this state of affairs. She talked him into taking on a partner. He took on several, but none of them was able to keep up with the workload, and they all dropped out after a few months.

On occasion I would get a ride with my father or with one of his partners to Tel Aviv or to Jerusalem. The experiences had one thing in common: At some point in the trip the driver would start dozing off behind the wheel. More than once I had to pinch the driver and shout in his ear to wake him up. One partner, named Deutsch, used to sing out loud to stay awake. I remember singing along with him, to help out. It was quite an experience. I also remember once on the road from Jerusalem seeing my father fall asleep and swerve off the road. Only by a miracle we did not end up at the bottom of the hill with the wheels of the truck up in the air. My father, of course, told me not to tell mother. but mother was no fool. She knew all about it.

And so again my parents began to bring up the issue of immmigrating to the United States, where my father would start a business, become more affluent, and start leading a normal life. My father's cousin in New York, Anna Tannenbaum, had arranged all the papers for us to immigrate to the United States, and we were now ready to go. But at the last minute my parents decided not to do it. It meant betraying their friends and their new state, which they had struggled so hard and so long to build. They just couldn't do it.

59.

Here, more or less, my story ends. The year 1950 was the end of the birth, even though twenty years later, in 1970, at the Hebrew University in Jerusalem, old man Ben-Gurion would tell a group of Reform rabbis from the United States, including yours truly, that the state of Israel was not yet fully there. Well, in a way, it may not yet be fully there for many years to come. But the critical question as to whether the birth was successful was, in my opinion, being answered in 1950. It would take a few more years and a few more wars, but what one may call the Manifest Destiny of the new state was clear by now. As for one of the children of the dream -- myself, for me there were three distinctive periods during the time of the birth: The first started on November 29, 1947, with the UN resolution on the partition of Palestine, and culminated in January 1949, with the signing of the cease-fire agreement with the belligerent Arab states. The second period was the rest of 1949, during which time the new state had to prove it could survive not only the onslaught of its enemies, but also such enemies as hunger, poverty, harsh weather, and conflicting cultures. When 1950 started, many of the problems had not yet gone away, but solutions were being worked out, and it was clear that the state was here to stay.

It was a thrill beyond words to be a witness at the creation. That eight-year-old boy knew that what he was witnessing was an event that happens perhaps once in a thousand years. In time, the events narrated in this memoir will become legends. They will take on biblical proportions, and will be given all sorts of lofty interpretations. It is my sincere hope that this book will help keep some of these things in their right perspective. I would like future generations to realize that, when all is said and done, we were ordinary people, living during a most unordinary time. We did what we could, but there must have been a higher force that determined the outcome. It is said that the Almighty takes away with one hand, and gives with the other. Never was this more true than during my own lifetime, when so much was taken away from us, and so much was given to us.

60.

After I started writing this book I went back to Haifa to the scenes of my childhood to find out how the city and the old neighborhoods look now, fifty years later. I have been back to Haifa over the years, but always for a short visit of a few hours, invariably to visit my uncle and aunt who lived in South America when the events narrated in this book took place, and settled in a suburb of Haifa called Neve Shaanan after the Six Day War.

Everyone I knew in 1948 had since moved to the newer suburbs, mostly on Mount Carmel -- Ahuza, Carmelia, Dania, the French Carmel, and so on. These are breathtaking mountain neighborhoods, beautiful white stone and cement houses bathed in greenery -- tall pine trees and other perennials and many flowering bushes, clinging to mountain slopes and cliffs overlooking the blue Mediterranean, gleaming in the late summer sun, with Acre in the distance on the other side of the bay, a coastline punctuated with the white chalk cliffs of Rosh Hanikra, where Israel ends and Lebanon starts, and the Mountains of Lebanon in the haze of the far horizon.

Feeling like William Butler Yates did upon sailing to Byzantium, I drove to Haifa from Tel Aviv -- my present day venue -- and parked my rented Peugeot a block away from Luntz and Sokolov, the corner where I lived in 1948.

My heart skipped a beat. It was a journey back in time. The old streets were buzzing with people and cars, but I felt invisible. Some people might have noticed a middle aged man in blue jeans and a black T-shirt and sandals, wearing dark glasses and a golf hat from Vail, Colorado, which, except for the purple color, resembled the *kova tembel,* the farmer's hat so popular in 1948. But no one saw the real me, the eight year old boy who was going back home, and no one had any notion I was communing with the sidewalks, the back yards, the shape of the streets running up and down the foothills of Mount Carmel, and the ghosts of the past.

Everything was now different. People no longer wore the simple khaki clothes of the time when Israel was born. They wore the same colorful shirts and pants and dresses I have seen in other places around the Mediterranean -- in Naples, in Saint Tropez, in Torre de Molinos. Haifa no longer was the city of pioneers it was back in 1948. It had become a Mediterranean city like all the others, only it spoke Hebrew. In point of fact, as I progressed (I use the word advisedly, since the streets were narrow and crowded) through the neighborhood I heard more Russian and Arabic than Hebrew. Arabic was spoken by Jews from neighboring Middle East countries, who constitute the majority of Israel's less affluent Jews, and who now live and work in my old neighborhood, which has long since become the low income part of town. Russian was spoken by the Jews who came from the former Soviet Union during the last two or three years. They too for the most part are now part of Israel's have-nots, and they live in the less affluent parts of the cities and towns. It was odd to hear those other languages spoken in the street. It took me back to 1948, when all or most of our parents were immigrants. Nothing changed in fifty years. Israel was still a country of newly-arrived immigrants.

I parked my car on Yalag Street (and later got a ticket for not putting the parking card on my car's side window), and walked towards Sokolov Street, which runs downhill from Herzl Street to the old Arab Lower Town, bordering on the Harbor. I started watching everything closely, trying to recapture the way things used to look. First I realized that the empty lot in front of me, on the corner of Sokolov and Hehalutz, where I often played as a child, was now occupied by a bulky, ugly gray stucco building, which turned out to be a movie theater, and which, to judge from the layers of grime on its walls, must have been there already for a good few years. That did not surprise me, since the population of Haifa more than tripled since I left that neighborhood in 1948, and since we Haifaites always had a passion for movies (no less than the Italian villagers depicted in that wonderful film, *Cinema Paradiso*). But then I turned down the street towards my old house on the corner of Sokolov and Luntz, and the scene that unfolded before me was quite incredible. The streets were lined up on both sides with fruit and vegetable stands, as well as nearly every other kind of food and household items and hardware. My old neighborhood had become one huge open air market stretching for blocks, down to Sirkin Street and up to Hehalutz and Yehiel Streets. In other words, the old Shuk Talpiot -- the indoor market housed in that old round building where my father used to work, which was around the corner from where we used to live, had spilled out into the streets and had become Haifa's outdoor market. All the places where I used to play, where my parents took walks, met their neighbors, went to the store, were now taken over by those stands, full of the smells and sounds of a marketplace.

It made me feel both happy and sad. I was happy to see all this life and vitality around me, new immigrants starting a new life where I once started mine, and availing themselves of the produce and products of their new homeland at prices they obviously could afford. But I was sad because what once was was now gone forever. All the old players seemed to have left this particular stage of life, replaced by others. And because people around me had little or no idea how it all started. And this, after all, may be the reason why I am writing this book, because I want them and everyone else who may some day

232

wonder how the state of Israel was born, to know about my old neighborhood, and other neighborhoods like it, which were the cradle in which the infant state saw the light of day.

But, as it turned out, I was too hasty in drawing the above conclusions. All the players were not gone, not even now, fifty years later. A few remained, and I soon ran into some of them. It started with a toy store on Herzl Street. I remembered it from my earliest childhood, when I first learned how to walk. I went inside and saw an old man reading a newspaper. In Israel people read newspapers religiously, as though their lives depend on it, which it does. I waited until he noticed my presence and asked him whether he was here in 1948. Yes, he was. He had owned this store for over fifty years. I told him I was one of his earliest costumers. My mother use to buy me metal tinker toys and tin soldiers when I was five or six, and his store was my favorite store in all of Herzl Street. He gave me a faint smile, and I could tell he wanted to get back to reading his newspaper.

But my biggest surprise awaited me when I went back to Sokolov Street, to look for that print shop, Amanut Press, where my mother worked when I was only three, when she used to take me every day to that preschool, or day care center, as we call it today, near Struck Park. I looked around but the print shop was gone. It then occurred to me that right next to it there used to be a barber shop, where I had my hair cut till we left the neighborhood in 1948. I looked around and, sure enough, there was the old barber shop, which had remained engraved in my memory all those years as the quintessential barber shop, the mother of all barber shops, the one which, albeit small and primitive, I have always compared all other barber shops to whenever and wherever I went for a haircut.

I went inside and found an old couple operating the place.

The old man, bald and stocky with a drooping Prussian mustache, was cutting another old man's hair, and the old woman, a bulky Haifa matron, was keeping an eye on two other old men who were waiting their turn. They both looked at me, wondering who this new client was. There was one empty chair in this small barbershop, and I sat down next to the two old men. The barber gave me a faint smile and told me it will only be a few minutes.

As I sat there I tried to recapture some of the associations this place evoked in my memory across the years. I found myself back in time, age six or seven, a wiry boy with blond hair in his khaki shorts and khaki shirt and brown leather sandals, looking at all those wonderful flasks of hair tonic and shampoo and all those brushes and combs and scissors, especially the serrated ones for thinning out one's hair. My heart was overcome with emotion. I was able to be two persons at the same time -- a six year old and a fifty-four year old, seeing the same things from two totally different perspectives, from the child's perspective of awe and wonderment, and from the old adult perspective of jaded experience and critical comparison, noticing the discomfort of the chair, the small quarters, the old fashioned barber tools, the untidy floor, and so on. And then and there I knew how much more intense, pure and wholesome are the feelings of childhood than anything we ever experience in later life, and why for the rest of our lives we are basically engaged in one activity -- a constant, ongoing attempt to recapture our childhood, to fulfill its dreams, and to dream those dreams one more time.

But this is not where the barber shop story ends. After I snapped out of my reverie I observed the interaction between the barber and his clients. I presently realized he hardly knew them, a strange fact considering it was a small neighborhood barber shop, where typically the barber knows his clients intimately, especially in a small city like Haifa, where people live for a long time in the same place. It didn't take me long to figure it out. They were all newly arrived Russian immigrants, who hardly spoke any Hebrew. They were too old to learn a new language, and since the barber did not speak Russian they communicated by gesturing and acting out words. The barber treated them with kindness, belying his bulky frame and Prussian expression. When he finished cutting their hair he would send them off with a *Shana Tova*, happy new year, since it was the week before Rosh Hashana.

It was now my turn to have my hair cut. I was invited to sit in the barber chair and was properly wrapped in a white apron tightly fitted around my neck. I proceeded to tell the barber I had my hair cut in this place fifty ears ago. At first he did not seem to grasp what I said. I repeated myself once or twice. He stopped to look at me with slow questioning eyes.

"Do I know you?"

"Were you here fifty years ago?"

"I certainly was. This year is my fiftieth anniversary here, and I am retiring after the holy days."

"My name is Mordecai Schreiber."

"Schreiber? What was your father's name?"

"Zvi."

"Zvi! I thought so!" He turned to the old woman. "Hannah, this is Zvi Schreiber's son! Remember him? Tall, strong, used to have a truck and transport the fish from the harbor to the market, where we used to go and buy fish for the Sabbath."

The old woman nodded her head without saying a word.

"My goodness," the old man said, his voice trembling with emotion. "Is your father still alive?"

"No, he passed away ten years ago."

The old barber looked down at his shoes, and I could tell he was holding back his tears. I must have taken him back in time to his younger days, and like myself, he was suddenly two persons, a young man and an old man, feeling the burden of the years.

After I left the barber shop, my hair much shorter than it was when I walked in, I wandered down Herzl Street, awash with a flood of memories. It was a strange sensation, walking down what used to be Haifa's main avenue, looking for the past. All around me people were going about their daily business, living in the present moment, while I was looking for something long gone, moving among them like an invisible man, like a ghost from the past, meeting other ghosts, seeing things which were no longer there, hearing voices and sounds which only existed in my memory.

It suddenly occurred to me that my past was linked to their present. Because of those years of war and struggle, which my parents' generation and mine went through back in 1948, all these Jews from Arab lands and from the former Soviet Union now had a home, a town by the sea where they were now rebuilding their lives, where, for the first time in centuries, they were not second class citizens, as my parents once were in Poland, but could walk tall and breathe the air of freedom and wear the uniform of the *Tzvah Hagana L'Yisrael*, the Jewish Defense Forces, and take their place among the nations of the world. And so I didn't mind being a ghost. I didn't mind the fact they didn't know me, and had no idea I was there at the creation, and played a part in it. It was not important. Long ago that mysterious fighter for Jewish freedom, Yair, referred in a poem to himself and his generation as "Anonymous Soldiers." We were, and we remain anonymous soldiers whose lives were dedicated to our people, for we did not

236

want to see our people suffer any longer. We wanted them to be once again a free people in their beautiful land, the land of Zion and Jerusalem. That was all we wanted, and here I was, fortunate enough to see for myself it all came true, and "the sons and daughters of Israel have returned home," and now "they are living under their vines and under their fig trees, and none shall make them afraid." And, let me tell you, walking up one of Haifa's streets I saw a most beautiful fig tree, and the ripe figs were falling down, bursting with honey, like small explosions on the sidewalk, and the vineyards on Mount Carmel, outside Zikhron Yaakov were groaning with grapes, and I knew without a doubt that when the prophet Isaiah spoke those words he had Haifa in mind.

61

Land of dreams. Even as a small child I was intoxicated by the incredible beauty of this land. I was taught in kindergarten that the purpose of our coming back to this land was to make the desert bloom. When my parents came here some 70 years earlier, much of this land was still desert. The great Sahara desert, which reaches into Egypt and the Sinai, claimed the entire south of our land, namely, the Negev, and reached as far north as the Galilee. Poor Mom and Dad, they had left a wooded and fertile Poland and came to a land of desert and swamps, of malaria and oppressive summer heat, and they sang,

> *Let the desert sing and rejoice,*
> *Let the prairie break into song,*
> *Let the wilderness bloom like the rose.*

Thus spoke the prophet Isaiah, and the present-day song-writer took the prophet's words and composed a stirring melody which the young pioneers sang and danced to as they made the desert bloom. In one settlement near the Dead Sea, called Beit Ha'aravah (home on the prairie), the ground was oversaturated with salt and minerals and could not grow a single blade of grass. So they dug up clods of soil and put them in a sieve and washed them with running water till the clods became usable for growing cucumbers and tomatoes. They put new life into the soil. They were out to prove that every acre of this land could be reclaimed for agriculture. And they were right. Isaiah certainly was right (a prophet in never wrong), and so were they. They were able to grow big luscious cucumbers and tomatoes, and even big red roses. (Today Israel has one of the most advanced cut flower industries in the world, mostly grown in the desert, which enjoy brisk sales in Europe). But in 1948 Beit Haaravah was overrun by the Arab Legion, and the kibbutz was abandoned. The surviving members of the kibbutz moved north, to the Galilee, and started a new farm under less austere conditions.

The love of the people for the land made the land more beautiful every year. People grow old, and lose their good looks as the years go by. Not so the land, into which the people have been pouring their life and their love. Now, fifty years later, the land is more beautiful than ever before, and its beauty grows with every passing day.

To illustrate my point, let's look at the desert town of Elat, where the Negev desert touches the Red Sea. In 1948, Elat was a small dormant Arab village. It was isolated from the outside world, and among the few Westerners who ever reached it was the legendary Lawrence of Arabia, who passed through the nearby town of Aqaba on his way to organizing the Arab Revolt, and the American Jewish archeologist, Nelson Glueck, who came down to look for King Solomon's copper mines at nearby Etzion Gever. In 1948 Elat became part of the new state of Israel. Jews began to settle there and build the town and its tourist industry. A small harbor was built to ship Israeli products to Asia and Africa. I first arrived in Elat in 1970. There were some small hotels, and a motor boat with glass panels installed on its bottom allowed tourists to see some of the tropical fish and coral reefs on the floor of the sea. During the seventies and eighties I went back several times, and watched the town grow and add five-star hotels, an international airport, and some international resorts, such as Club Med. I was able to do some snorkeling as well as scuba diving, and see some of the most beautiful marine life in the world. But it was not until September, 1993, that I saw the full beauty of Elat, and its great natural resources. It has become one of the most developed and breathtaking resorts in the world. Plane-loads of sun-seeking Scandinavian and German tourists were arriving every day. My wife and I were fortunate enough to stay in a new hotel near the Egyptian border called The Princess, one of the most luxurious hotels and one of the most beautiful feats of architecture I have ever seen, a glass and marble palace built into the mountain and perched over the deep blue waters of the Red Sea (please note that there is nothing "red" about this sea. It was originally called the "Sea of Reeds," because of the papyrus reeds which grow at its other end in Egypt, and somehow the name was changed in English from "reed" to "red"). This time we took a boat to Pharaoh Island in Egyptian territorial waters, along with a group of tourists from all over the world, and did some of the best diving I have ever done. And even more to the point, we visited some relatives from Brooklyn who had made Elat their home back in the sixties, and found out from the father of the family, a marine biologist, all about fish farming in Elat, a major source of fresh fish, and it made me think of my own father and his friends who started the fish industry in Israel some sixty years earlier, up north in Haifa, on the Mediterranean Sea. And somehow, notwithstanding all that progress, one could clearly feel that "the best is yet to come."

62.

And so, even now, fifty years later, Israel is still being born. Every day, when new immigrants arrive at Ben-Gurion Airport or at the Haifa harbor, a new beginning is occasioned by their arrival. And now I know, beyond a shadow of a doubt, that many more will arrive. For as time goes on, it becomes clearer and clearer that the Jewish heart and the Jewish soul have only one home -- this wondrous land that begins where the Jordan River originates, in the northern mountains, and ends where the Red Sea starts, in Elat, where Asia and Africa meet.

For this is not an ordinary land. Its hills and valleys speak an ancient tongue, a tongue which Jews as well as Christians and Moslems believe is the language of God. From the origins of the Jordan to the shores of the Red Sea there is no escaping this tongue. Every stone and every grain of sand in this land is associated with it, and seems to whisper words from the Book of Books, which was written in this land. This land holds sway over people unlike any other place in the world. And this is why so many nations have tried to make this land their own. But in the end they all failed, because long ago God promised Abraham, "To you and to your descendants have I promised this land." This is why, despite the fact that for some twenty centuries Abraham's children were banished from this land, they are now coming back, millions of them, and more millions will come.

We Jews are in love with this land. It is an endless love story. It began when God said to Abraham, *Lech lecha*, go forth, leave you home in Babylonia, and go to the land that I will show you. And it has continued for nearly four thousand years, through wars and famine and incredible suffering. My own definition of who is a Jew is: A Jew is someone who is deeply in love with the Land of Israel. It was God's will for us to love the

Land of Israel. And, I wonder -- has any love ever been put to greater tests than our love for this land? Israel, indeed, was born out of the greatest test of all, the Holocaust in Europe. They shot us and burned us and killed us with lethal gas by the millions, but they did not break our spirit. And the few of us who survived rose against new enemies who came at us from all sides and routed them, and we flung the gates of this land wide open to our brothers and sisters from all the corners of the earth, and when they arrive at Haifa harbor and at Ben-Gurion Airport we are always reminded of that love, we see it in their eyes, and in their quickening heartbeat, and when they fall down on the ground and kiss it, like a man kisses his beloved:

For I betroth you unto me in love, and faith, and mercy, and you will know your Lord.